Con Artists in Cinema

This book examines the con artist film as a genre, exploring its main features while also addressing variations within it.

The volume explores three diverse themes of the con artist film: edification, self-awareness, and liberation through con games; the femme fatale as con artist; and romantic love as a plot point. Analyzing movies such as *Matchstick Men* (2003), *House of Games* (1987), *Body Heat* (1981), *The Last Seduction* (1994), *Birthday Girl* (2001), and *The Game* (1997), the book also explores their psychological investigation of the con artist figure, the con artist's mark, and how the dynamic between these roles implicates us as the audience. It also addresses the con artist film genre's close association with neo-noir, especially through the femme fatale figure, investigating and updating the rich tradition of noir film.

Demonstrating the range and flexibility of this understudied genre, this book will be of interest to scholars and students of film studies, ethics, and those studying the representation of women in film.

Joseph H. Kupfer is University Professor of Philosophy at Iowa State University, USA.

Routledge Focus on Film Studies

1 Robot Ecology and the Science Fiction Film
J. P. Telotte

2 Weimar Cinema, Embodiment, and Historicity
Cultural Memory and the Historical Films of Ernst Lubitsch
Mason Kamana Allred

3 Migrants in Contemporary Spanish Film
Clara Guillén Marín

4 Virtue and Vice in Popular Film
Joseph H. Kupfer

5 Unproduction Studies and the American Film Industry
James Fenwick

6 Indian Indies
A Guide to New Independent Indian Cinema
Ashvin Immanuel Devasundaram

7 Migration and Identity in British East and Southeast Asian Cinema
Leung Wing-Fai

8 Con Artists in Cinema
Self-Knowledge, Female Power, and Love
Joseph H. Kupfer

Con Artists in Cinema
Self-Knowledge, Female Power, and Love

Joseph H. Kupfer

LONDON AND NEW YORK

First published 2024
by Routledge
4 Park Square, Milton Park, Abingdon, Oxon OX14 4RN

and by Routledge
605 Third Avenue, New York, NY 10158

Routledge is an imprint of the Taylor & Francis Group, an informa business

© 2024 Joseph H. Kupfer

The right of Joseph H. Kupfer to be identified as author of this work has been asserted in accordance with sections 77 and 78 of the Copyright, Designs and Patents Act 1988.

All rights reserved. No part of this book may be reprinted or reproduced or utilised in any form or by any electronic, mechanical, or other means, now known or hereafter invented, including photocopying and recording, or in any information storage or retrieval system, without permission in writing from the publishers.

Trademark notice: Product or corporate names may be trademarks or registered trademarks, and are used only for identification and explanation without intent to infringe.

British Library Cataloguing-in-Publication Data
A catalogue record for this book is available from the British Library

Library of Congress Cataloging-in-Publication Data
Names: Kupfer, Joseph H., author.
Title: Con artists in cinema : self-knowledge, female power, and love /
Joseph H. Kupfer.
Description: New York : Routledge, 2024. |
Series: Routledge focus on film studies | Includes bibliographical references and index. |
Identifiers: LCCN 2023016070 (print) | LCCN 2023016071 (ebook) |
Subjects: LCSH: Swindlers and swindling in motion pictures.
Classification: LCC PN1995.9.S95 K87 2024 (print) | LCC PN1995.9.S95
(ebook) | DDC 791.43/6556—dc23/eng/20240501
LC record available at https://lccn.loc.gov/2023016070
LC ebook record available at https://lccn.loc.gov/2023016071

ISBN: 978-1-032-42187-2 (hbk)
ISBN: 978-1-032-42846-8 (pbk)
ISBN: 978-1-003-36454-2 (ebk)

DOI: 10.4324/9781003364542

Typeset in Times New Roman
by codeMantra

For My Wonderful Colleagues at Iowa State University

Contents

	Introduction	1
1	Con Artist's Comeuppance and Cure: *Matchstick Men*	10
2	Revenge and Self-Knowledge: *House of Games*	21
3	The Femme Fatale as Con Artist: *Body Heat*	33
4	Improvising on the Run: *The Last Seduction*	49
5	Con Game as Prelude to Love: *Birthday Girl*	62
6	*The Game* of Brotherly Love	77
	Index	*89*

Introduction

The Genre

Films about con artists or confidence men constitute a popular, worldwide genre, yet one that has not received sustained analysis the way westerns, horror films, or romantic comedies, for example, have. This book is in part inspired by Stanley Cavell's *Pursuits of Happiness*, in which he captures and dissects a genre of film: the Hollywood comedy of remarriage. His landmark book, which arguably inaugurated a whole field of philosophical scholarship, examined movies we had long enjoyed but had not considered a distinctive group. I do not presume to do for movies about con artists what Cavell does for the comedies he organizes and analyzes. For one, I do not possess Cavell's incredible powers of appreciation and discrimination, nor do I have his flair for writing with such insight and erudition. I am simply trying to call attention to some interesting and revealing features about a genre that does not seem to have received the careful scrutiny it deserves.

Even as Cavell's book characterizes the structure of the remarriage genre, so does it plumb their differences. My book about con artists similarly explores the main features of con artist films while addressing important variations within them. Rather than stipulate conditions or features that are essential to the genre, I will offer a broad characterization, aiming to capture what we might consider typical of these films. After which I will explain why certain films or their type fall outside my interest, if not strict understanding. The variations include films that incorporate novel elements, such as female con artists and confidence men who themselves are the victims of flimflam. What emerges is an appreciation for the range of the genre, admitting in-depth treatment of such diverse themes as edification through con games, the femme fatale as con artist, and how love can be pivotal to con games. The con artist film is enjoyable in itself; it is like a "whodunit," only replacing the perpetrator of the crime as its focus with how it is accomplished, a "howdunit." The subject of the con artist film is a form of crime, theft of money, emphasizing cunning and theatrics, always executed with disguise and deception. Dissecting the genre includes examining the intricacies of the "game:" its design and how it entraps its victim. We also savor anticipating whether the con will

DOI: 10.4324/9781003364542-1

2   *Introduction*

succeed and sometimes rooting for the con man, especially if he is trying to best someone who is clearly himself unlikable or downright criminal.

The con artist story makes the play central, perhaps rivaling the lucrative payoff as an attraction for the hucksters. In keeping with the familiar phrase "con game," the con artist takes pleasure and pride in playing a game: making the right moves, outmaneuvering his victims, and coming out victorious. But the theatrical play also looms large, as the cohort of con men "put on a play." As in legitimate dramaturgy, the director of the ploy stages it – sometimes with a variety of scenes, replete with convincing props. Members of the devious troupe assume characters in the charade and follow a script, yet improvise as circumstances may require. The ability to think on their feet is essential to the grifters because their marks occasionally deviate from what is expected or something unforeseen occurs that requires immediate alteration of the planned ploy. Timing is critical as the players synchronize their entrances and exits, attuned to one another as well as to the reactions of their victims. The con as dramatic play comports with flimflam men viewing themselves as "artists," as Roy (in our film, *Matchstick Men*) makes explicit when explaining his work to his alleged daughter. Whether the play of a game or theatre, the cheating gambit also includes risk, adding suspense and excitement to the venture. Even a small monetary gain, therefore, can yield considerable ancillary pleasure.

In all the movies I have chosen, the audience discovers the con at the same time as its victim, who is usually, though not always, also the movie's protagonist. We might, then, consider such plots "surprise" con games, since the revelation of what has been transpiring throws us psychologically off-balance, amusing us with its unexpected turn of events. It seems fair to say that the film itself partakes of the con. Making us into accompanying or implicit dupes, the con game becomes imminent: immediate in our own experience. This identification with the patsy makes the grift more vivid and plausible. Providing us with a powerful lesson in conning, we are less likely to feel superior to the dupe in the story. After all, we cannot look down on the victim who has suffered at the hands of the con artist if we are in the same unexpected position he or she has been lured into. And this adds to the credibility of the plot.

Such surprise flimflam films contrast with those in which we are shown the workings of the con game while the gull remains in the dark. Paradigmatic among such films, of course, is *The Sting* (George Roy Hill, 1973). In this memorable movie, we are let in on the construction of the con and its well-appointed set, the roles of the con men and their props, potential dangers run, and the huge, desirable payoff. *The Sting* situates us amid the likable grifters, as if we are part of their coterie. We enjoy the buildup to the big payday, especially since the mark has been shown to be venal and greedy. Fleecing him, therefore, does not feel in the least reprehensible and that enhances the thrill of the game. The flawed character of the victim in *The Sting* points to

Introduction 3

an underlying insight of the genre: marks are typically not wholly innocent. They are often susceptible to the con artist's gambits because of some moral weakness of their own, such as greed. The prospect of unearned financial gain motivates the grifter's typical targets, and this less than kosher purpose leaves them exposed to the con man's machinations. The moral deficiencies of the mark may, then, feel to viewers something like a minor permission to relish the ingenuity of the con game as well as the deftness of the con artist in pulling it off.

What exactly should count as a con artist film is open to interpretation and disagreement. Some viewers might well consider such grand cinematic impostors as Tom Ripley (Matt Damon) in *The Talented Mr. Ripley* (Anthony Minghella, 1999) and Frank Abagnale, Jr. (Leonardo DiCaprio) in Steven Spielberg's *Catch Me If You Can* (2002) as con artists supreme. These characters certainly fool people and engage in fabulous role play: Ripley's prolonged charade as Dickie Greenleaf and Abagnale's serial professional occupations. But for me, these are more lavish impersonations rather than genuine grifts. What is missing from the actions of both characters is a scripted scheme that deceives people in order to rob them. The professional con man performs in episodic ventures exploiting different marks or gulls with a variety of ploys.

Ripley and Abagnale pretend to be someone or something they are not. They concoct no game and put on no play or skit. They do not entrap someone into emptying their bank accounts. Neither Ripley nor Abagnale has a clear victim or designated sucker; instead, the whole world is being deceived as they go about their business. It is true that in our movie *Body Heat* (Lawrence Kasdan, 1981), Matty is an impersonator; her real name is MaryAnn, she assumes the name and identity of a former classmate. However, Matty's impersonation of the real Matty is minimalist (especially as compared with Ripley's and Abagnale's) and is merely a moving part of a complex and extended con game. Her grift involves further subterfuge and trickery and eventuates with the theft of a huge inheritance as well as framing her paramour/chump for the climactic murder. In these important respects, then, her impersonation diverges from those of the noteworthy male movie frauds.

Here, we might wish to consider the humorous and morally uplifting impersonation that is the premise of Ivan Reitman's film *Dave* (1993). An ordinary citizen, Dave Kovic (Kevin Kline) winds up pretending to be his look-alike president after the latter suffers a debilitating stroke. Although part of a nefarious plot of a wicked official in the government, Dave himself is hardly a con artist looking to make a killing. As with Ripley, Dave's stint playing the part of someone he is not is long-lasting and deceives everyone, but Dave's lack of larceny pushes his pretense even further away from that of classic con artists. Perhaps this trio of films and others like them are better viewed as stories that are more about protracted role play, occupying a place alongside con game movies in their shared outlandish approach to credulity.

4   *Introduction*

Pervasive Themes

Three powerful themes run through most if not all of the films discussed in this book: romantic love, violence, and self-knowledge. The films are evenly divided in depicting romantic love in its false guise, employed by the grifters as an ingredient to their plan to swindle the dupe, and presenting love as a genuine possibility for the mark of the con game. As you would expect, the spurious occurrences of romantic interest are a way to play on the gull's sexual desire or loneliness. The femmes fatales in our middle pair of films obviously and convincingly use their erotic charms to inveigle their would-be paramours into killing their husbands. In this respect, the deadly woman reprises the classic role that helped shape movies during the heyday of *film noir*, in the 1940s and early 1950s. In our films, the dark mistress also seems to take pleasure in her sexual liaison: both the physical intimacy and also her dominance in controlling its instigation and continuation. In our second film, the main male con artist uses romantic interest to further entrap his female victim. When she later overhears him chortling about their sexual interlude as a sacrifice for the sake of the ploy to steal her money, she is humiliated as much by the amorous deception as by being taken for her economic fortune.

In other films, romantic connection is held out as a hopeful conclusion to the story. It is an unforeseen, serendipitous blessing of being the target of the con. The last pair of films along with our initial movie offer genuine romance as a worthwhile outcome, sometimes compensating the mark for being ripped off, sometimes merely a tangential unfolding after the victim has gotten over his ordeal. The films suggest that being played by the con game may, in fact, have "prepared" the protagonist/gull for the romantic possibility. In the three films that end on this upbeat note, the mark is a lonely man. The upending of his life by suffering the devastation of flimflam forces him into social interactions that directly or indirectly change him for the better. The social connecting, missing before being embroiled in the con game, readies the dupe for a new beginning, one that turns on an amorous relationship. Here, the story of *Birthday Girl* (Jez Butterworth, 2001) is striking. It presents both types of portrayals of romantic love in the con game films; the fake and the real amorous attachment are fused. What begins as a scam to lure the needy male mark into the grift evolves into the burgeoning of a true romantic coupling. The turbulence spun by the con game deepens the victim's relationship with the female grifter so that by the story's finale he is willing to completely shed his old life and embark on a caring relationship with the comely, but deceitful former foe.

As with romantic love, violence, both illusory and actual, fills the films I discuss. Consequently, they prod us to think about the relationship between con games and violence. In all but one of our films, the illusion or false attribution of violence is deployed as part of a con game. And in all but one of our films, actual violence either results from the con or is part of it. In an ideal grift, we might speculate, real violence would not be needed; its mere

Introduction 5

appearance or simulation should suffice. The sense we get from many con artists is that they intentionally spurn violence, being above its crude and obvious methods. After all, the con is clever and supplants the brutality of mayhem with quick-wittedness, dissembling, and intricate planning. Shooting, stabbing, punching, and clubbing would be for those who lack the inventiveness needed for the con. And yet, con artists often resort to the façade of violence or employ it if only in measured doses as part of the intricate theft.

The suggestion I offer is that despite being an ostensible, more ingenious alternative to violence, flimflam nevertheless relies on it, either in appearance or actuality. Even when con games completely avoid violence, the thrum and threat of it courses beneath the charade. Why should this be? Here are a couple of conjectures. First, there are the dangers that the con man risks should the mark see through his deception. For example, when the mark susses out the con in the film *Derailed* (Mikael Hafstrom, 2005), he unleashes a torrent of bloodshed. Swindling people opens the door to unforeseen and often uncontainable mayhem. A similar scenario is staged in our first film, with another Roy, in order to trick him out of his life's savings. The episodes of genuine and fake violence indicate that working con games can be a risky business.

But con games also resonate more deeply and subtly with physical harm. The theft through cleverly wrought deception violates the mark just as surely as outright violence does. In fact, there may be something more insidious in the "soft landing" created by the grift, with its patina of civility. In our film *Birthday Girl*, for example, John Buckingham thoughtfully indicts the female con artist who has toyed with him sexually in order to exploit him financially; he tells her that she has shredded his dignity. Playing upon the victim's desires and trust is a more subtle but perhaps more wounding attack on a person's self-respect than simply overpowering him or maiming him through violence. The con game uses the gull's distinctively human endowments against himself, exposing his personal weaknesses and stripping him of self-respect. This dynamic helps account for the eruption of violence from the female mark in David Manet's *House of Games* (1987) when she uncovers the truth hidden in her dalliance with con artists and their attractive ringleader. The films examined here will deepen our appreciation for the affinity between violence and con games: how physical brutality is put to use in the various swindles and why it lurks in the shadows of the con.

The acquisition of self-knowledge as a consequence of being conned is yet another of our pervasive themes. It is explicit in the first and third pair of the films. Being victimized by a grifting gambit is shown to be a force for introspection, encouraging the marks to confront their true natures and what is missing from their lives. As a result, the victims of their respective cons make existential changes in their lives, for the better. The implication is that being the target of a grift tears away the habitual ways the victims of the theft behave and see themselves; they are existentially bared to themselves as the interests that had obscured the individuals from themselves, such as work and wealth,

6 *Introduction*

are subordinated to the helter-skelter of the con game. Usually, this salutary upshot is but an unforeseen and unintended byproduct of the flimflam; the con artists are interested in making a haul, not in benefitting their sucker. However, in our concluding film, such self-assessment and lifestyle correction by the victim of the con game is actually the goal of its perpetrator.

Although not as obvious in the femmes fatales films, there is reason to believe that in the end, the paramour/dupes also achieve a modicum of gain in self-understanding. In our middle pair of films, the deadly women abscond with all the money, leaving their erstwhile lovers to molder in prison. Being the gull of their former love interest does not obviously seem to evoke the sort of self-evaluation that is the hallmark of the films in the other sections. Nevertheless, the conclusions of the stories suggest that their incarceration has indeed led the chumps to reflect on how they landed in the sad predicament in which they find themselves. At the very least, they realize how their sexual desires and amorous fantasies have made them vulnerable to women who, they must concede, are smarter and more insightful than they are. As they unravel the con games the women have played on them, the men seem to see how the vixens they thought took them seriously were merely using them to take the fall for their larceny.

Structure of the Presentation

The six films examined in the book are arranged in three sets of pairs. Each set focuses on a salient topic around which meaning in the two films coalesces. The three topics, so very different in nature, illustrate how supple the genre is in treating such varied issues within its recognizable lineaments. I believe this paired ordering is also helpful in that it deepens our understanding of how the films diverge, even as they explore the same issues within the boundaries of con artist stories.

Liberation Through Victimization

When successful, con games result in the enrichment of the con artists and monetary loss for their dupes. Two interesting inversions of the standard storyline enliven our first set of films. Both films include detailed instruction on running con games; however, the bigger lessons come in the form of increased self-knowledge and change of life as a result of being exploited by an extended, intricate con game. First, for an individual who is himself a seasoned grifter; next, for a mark who has been lured into the shady world of professional con artists. The self-knowledge, in turn, liberates the protagonists in the film stories ushering them into radically new lives. In the first, a con game is (ironically) visited on a con artist but he unexpectedly benefits greatly from being played for a sucker; his conscience-laden obsessive-compulsive

Introduction 7

behaviors evaporate. In the second, the con man is found out and must pay a heavy price; nevertheless, his victim gains from what she discovers about her deeper, darker nature, albeit in a criminal manner.

Women and Larceny: The Femme Fatale as Con Artist

Films about con games invariably feature men as the scheming mastermind. When women are involved, they are auxiliaries, helping to fashion the plot with which the con artist ensnares his prey. Consequently, films in which women are the con artist are instructively positioned to offer a different angle on con games.[1] The second category of films concerns femme fatales, women who seduce men into killing their husbands (as in classical *film noir*) but employ flimflam to do so. Where the original femmes fatales had only their erotic charms with which to wield power, the neo-noir species supplements her sexual force with brainy schemes. The upshot is that although such iconic femmes fatales as Barbara Stanwyck's Phyllis Dietrichson (*Double Indmenity,* Billy Wilder, 1944) ultimately fail in their murderous plan, our modern femmes fatales get away with the loot, scot free. These films also represent the ways in which the levers of legitimate power – social, financial, and legal – are denied even contemporary women. Wielding sexually charged con games is a way for such women to compete and vanquish the men who mistakenly think they are in charge.

Love and Deception

The third category turns on love: first, the potential for romantic love as the conclusion of the con game story and, then, love as the instigator of the convoluted plot. Con games are rarely a prelude to romantic interest, although the pretense of romance can certainly be part of the charade. In the first film of this pair, the romantic denouement actually plays ironically off the film's con game because it is the pursuit of a Russian bride that draws the protagonist/mark into the web of the cheating plan of the Russian grifters. Unlike our other films, the revelation of the con occurs midway through the story rather than in its conclusion, and this leaves room for us to be pleasantly surprised at the amorous finale. The second movie offers an interesting twist on the plotline of the genre by employing a con game to show someone that we care about them. Unlike typical con games, this one seeks to give something worthwhile to the victim instead of bilking him out of his money. As a result of his brother's ersatz flimflam, and the illusion of losing his fortune, the protagonist/dupe is jolted into reevaluating his wealth-saturated life and priorities. With its restorative purpose, the turmoil and dangers of the con game express love for the individual who is bedeviled by the game's fabrications.

8 *Introduction*

Reconfiguring the Genre

Among the reasons for choosing the films that I have is the impressive ways in which most of them make fundamental alterations to the typical or standard con artist tale. The first film, *Matchstick Men*, upends the genre by situating an established, successful con man as the mark. Although we are surprised at the con game revelation in all of our movies, this one is especially startling because a grifter seems the last character to be taken for a ride.[2] The movie also strikes a serious moral note by balancing the exploitation of the matchstick man with a happy ending for him. Being victimized by his long-time partner in crime actually cures the protagonist of his anxieties and compulsions, freeing him to pursue a loving relationship with a woman he has met, in part, because of the con game itself. The loss of his money through his partner's betrayal, then, yields a gain in worldly adjustment and happiness.

Our central cinematic duo reworks the genre in several distinctive ways. First, as noted, they cast women as the masterminds of the con. In elevating women to the major role, these films also make their viewpoint and interests central, whereas the usual setup nestles the audience in the life and viewpoint of the mark, now it is the con woman who functions as the story's protagonist. And, this is a reorientation in viewing perspective. These movies are also innovative in synthesizing the con game genre with the neo-noir version of the old-fashioned femmes fatales films of 1940s and 1950s. The films in our second section dress the con artists in the alluring curves of the deadly spider woman. Although the iconic femmes fatales of yesteryear did manage to do away with their husbands, they did not succeed in living happily ever after with the money (or the lovers who helped them pull of the murder). Armed with their brainy con games, however, the modern femmes fatales do indeed succeed; they make off with the loot and leave their accomplice/gulls in the lurch, to take the rap. In wedding the femme fatale tale to the con game genre, the films also make a subtle moral modification. In classic noir, the husbands to be dispatched were merely stodgy or boring, but in our neo-noir incarnations, they are themselves morally blemished. The moral turpitude of the murdered spouses may then serve to mitigate to some extent the evil of the fatal con games that their wives play on them, clearing emotional space for us to appreciate the cinematic cunning of these attractive but dodgy women.

The concluding film in our group offers yet another creative variation on the genre of grift. In this film, the scheme that appears to be a con game, to the protagonist as well as us in the audience, is itself a sham! The putative mark is himself fooled into thinking that he has lost all his fabulous wealth through an elaborate bit of flimflam. The deception about the game is enhanced by the grace note of having his "guide" in the proceedings announce that "it's a con!" Because he is fooled into thinking that he has been victimized by a con game, we can consider the story itself a "meta-con game"; a yarn whose purpose is to create the illusion of a grift when all is, in fact, benign is fooling the would-be

Introduction 9

gull and the audience about being conned. And surely, this sham scam is itself a novelty in the genre of film flimflam.

Con game films have intrigued and entertained audiences over many years and in a variety of cultures. And yet, the films have not received the careful attention they warrant. The discussions that follow try to sketch what makes con artist films a distinctive delight, especially those for which the audience is as taken aback by the revelation of the grift as the mark is. Explaining the genre's defining characteristics is complemented by articulating variations within the genre and demonstrating the range or elasticity of themes in its corpus. Among the variations explored are the con artist himself being the sucker of the scam, genuine transformation, women running the con, and the con game not resulting in the usual theft of money. The topics and themes of the con artist film can go in directions that are themselves as unexpected as the con game itself. Consequently, such topics as liberation through con game victimization and themes such as romantic love illustrate the way in which the genre's suppleness adds a dimension of enjoyment to its serpentine allure.

Notes

1 Some may put the Stanwyck character of Jean Harrington in Preston Sturges's *The Lady Eve* (1941) in the group of female con artists. Although somewhat plausible, I do not include card sharps or hustlers of various stripes as true grifters. They are simple cheats, not engaged in hatching a developed narrative, playing flexible roles, or fabricating game-like deceptions.
2 The wonderful Argentinian film *Nine Queens* (Fabian Bielinsky, 2000) also surprises by playing a delectable con on a professional grifter.

Bibliography

Cavell, Stanley (1981). *Pursuits of Happiness: The Hollywood Comedy of Remarriage.* Cambridge, MA: Harvard University.

Filmography

Bielinsky, Fabian (2000). *Nine Queens.* Argentina.
Butterworth, Jez (2001). *Birthday Girl.* U.S.
Frears, Stephen (1990). *The Grifters.* U.S.
Hafstrom, Mikael (2005). *Derailed.* U.S.
Hill, George Roy (1973). *The Sting.* U.S.
Kasdan, Lawrence (1981). *Body Heat.* U.S.
Mamet, David (1987). *House of Games.* U.S.
Minhella, Anthony (1999). *The Talented Mr. Ripley.* U.S.
Reitman, Ivan (193). *Dave.* U.S.
Scott, Ridley (2003). *Matchstick Men.* U.S.
Spielberg, Steven (2002). *Catch Me If You Can.* U.S.
Wilder, Billy (1944). *Double Indemnity.* U.S.

1 Con Artist's Comeuppance and Cure

Matchstick Men

Con Game Tutorials

For all its deftness with con games, in all sizes, *Matchstick Men* (Ridley Scott, 2003) is at the bottom about morality and happiness, and the connection between them. The protagonist's original situation and psychology undergo a radical, but salutary, alteration as a result of a life-changing con played on him. The film takes great pains to establish who Roy Waller (Nicolas Cage) is at the story's beginning, including his serious flaws, and to contrast this with a meliorating conclusion. In doing so, the film situates the audience in the perspective of Roy, a seasoned con man, who nevertheless is the victim of a superior con sprung on him by his long-time partner in slippery crime. We, in the audience, are pulled along as the scheme that ensnares Roy unfolds; consequently, we are as surprised as he is to discover his fate as a mark of the still more devious grifter with whom he has long teamed up. And this deviates from the usual plot in the genre: we rarely find that the major scam is visited on a con man.[1] Making us into accompanying dupes, we identify with Roy. Our identification with the grifter cum chump makes con games themselves more palpable and believable; after all, if we can be fooled, the manipulation of marks so as to empty their pockets is not terribly far-fetched.

To this implicit, imminent lesson in trickery, the film adds explicit tutorials in the art of the flimflam. Roy instructs his would-be daughter (Angela, Alison Lohman) in the niceties of the "short con."[2] We, in the audience, learn about the craft: the structure of particular tricks or "gaffs," the psychological interaction between con artist and his gull, and varieties of deceit. Participation by the eager student is essential to the ultimate con that is perpetrated on Roy himself. As with most, if not all, flimflam scams, these intricate schemes have as their purpose the theft of the marks' money.

But the film also buttresses this business side of conning with the delights of its playful aspects. The story underscores the satisfaction to be derived from playing the con, staging a "game." The entire charade is something like a theatrical play, replete with script, roles, occasionally sets, dramatic actions, and climactic finale. In addition to the benefit of now possessing the mark's

DOI: 10.4324/9781003364542-2

Con Artist's Comeuppance and Cure: Matchstick Men   11

money, the con artists enjoy the manipulation and deception requisite to making the grift work. The con man also takes pride in his cunning: thinking up the ploy, engaging and fooling his victims, and realizing the payoff. Roy is adept at sharing this playful aspect of con with Angela and her enthusiastic response draws him further into the con game that is being woven around him. When working with his partner, Frank (Sam Rockwell), Roy follows a script they have crafted but is alert to the need to improvise as a change in the situation or the behavior of the gulls warrants. Timing is critical as the grifters establish a tempo in their deceitful lines and dissembling actions; Roy and Frank, and now Angela, must respond to each other as well as to the reactions of their victims. The con as larcenous theatre is reinforced by matchstick men viewing themselves as "artists." Roy emphasizes the craftmanship that informs apparently simple acts of deception when reluctantly explaining his work at the insistence of Roy's impostor daughter, Angela. Cheating people out of their money also puts the con artist at risk, which adds the frisson of danger to the proceedings. And as the con that entraps Roy unfolds, he is exposed to unforeseen harm.

Besides play, two further, more ominous themes are explored in the film. One is the cost the con men pay for their deceptive vocations. This is most apparent in the amusing but disconcerting tics and rituals exhibited by Roy, but perhaps is also responsible for the apparent emptiness of his life.[3] Aside from his partner, Frank, Roy has no friends and no interests outside his money-making schemes. For that matter, we never see Frank enjoying a life outside his grifting profession. The other theme is the presence of violence – feigned, latent, and overtly destructive.

As in many con game films, sham violence is integral to the major con played on Roy.[4] The movie encourages us to consider the relationship between violence and grifting. After all, the con game is notable as a way of using wiles instead of actual violence or its threat to extract money from a dupe. The best cons, moreover, conceal themselves from their victims so that they never realize that they have been taken and this, too (the "blow off"), often turns upon the appearance of mayhem. Such ignorance keeps suckers from seeking redress, either through official legal channels or by dint of their own devices. However, the pretenses of violence that are often ingredient to the games con men play seem to vibrate with the dangers of genuine violence. Should the scheme backfire, we wonder, would the con artists suffer serious harm? This intimation is brought home forcefully, for example, when (another) Roy is struck with a bat in the abdomen by an alert bar man who discerns Roy's attempt at sleight-of-hand with money of different denominations in *The Grifters.* In *Matchstick Men*, Roy does, in fact, suffer actual physical damage, but it is integral to the structure of the con game being worked on him.

We initially see Roy and his partner, Frank, pull off a modest but slick scam on a married couple who think they have won a prize but who are soon tricked into providing their bank account number to the hustling duo. We are

12   *Con Artist's Comeuppance and Cure:* Matchstick Men

amused, but perhaps a bit disturbed, by the tics and quirky repetitions that accompany and manifest Roy's obsessive-compulsiveness. Obviously anxious and painfully neat, we do not see the root of Roy's troubled behavior and psychological handicaps in his devious work until the conclusion of the film story, when they completely disappear.

Roy lives in a comfortable home, but it is bland, bordering on the sterile. The lack of vibrancy or individuality in his home is a physical representation of the paucity of his social, personal life. Aside from his grifting sidekick, Frank, Roy has no friends or even acquaintances. In addition, he seems consumed by his work; he does nothing besides conning people: no hobbies, interests, and pastimes. In other words, Roy's life is narrow and pretty barren, until he is lured into the machinations of the uber con man. It is ironic that Roy's life actually becomes richer as a result of becoming the gull of the devastating con game Frank cooks up. The joys of his relationship with his would-be daughter, pivotal to the trick being played on him, underline the social emptiness of Roy's life. The newfound relationship with Angela adds appreciably to his lackluster personal life, even as it serves to embroil him in the fraudulent web that will cost him dearly.

The Malaise of Roy's Malevolence

From the outset of *Matchstick Men*, Roy seems unwell: he enters and leaves his house counting to three (sometimes in Spanish); he punctuates his movements with a humming grunt and eye twitches; he takes what are purported to be anti-anxiety pills. He will repeat "pygmies" when something distressing occurs. Roy's home, replete with a sparkling blue swimming pool, is upscale and spacious, but devoid of any personality. After Roy and his partner, Frank, complete a con game begun over the phone, Roy makes woofing noises and, through his eyes, we see bright images flicker and jump. Frank accuses Roy of not taking his pills. We soon watch Roy appearing to subsist on cigarettes and canned tuna, the remnants of which he meticulously disposes. He then cleans his home excessively as a way of coping with the loss of his anti-anxiety pills, coupled with the unexpected departure of his doctor. The array of twitches and hitches, grunts and incantations cycles through the movie – humorously but darkly. Only at the story's end do we understand them for the occupational hazards they are.

The obsessive-compulsive affliction should give us pause. It is indicative of someone who feels out of control; the ritualistic repetitions provide a semblance of order but do not truly address the individual's sense of precariousness. Roy's clean, neat, and tidy home further attests to his fixation on controlling what he can, here, his environment. However, the con man is a paradigm of someone who is in control. He orchestrates a crisp (short con) or elaborate (long con) scheme through which he manipulates his mark at his

Con Artist's Comeuppance and Cure: Matchstick Men   13

whim in order to fleece him. The matchstick man is in charge and reaps his pecuniary reward as a result. Roy has been very good at this, as evidenced by his sizable stash of money as well as his comfortable home. So at least for Roy, the deception, manipulation, and ensuing larceny undermine his feeling of command. Deviating as he does from morality makes him feel unmoored, regardless of apparent outward control of events. Since the same cannot be said for Roy's partner, Frank, or other of our cinematic grifters, we are forced to conclude that Roy is the outlier: a con man with a conscience. Violating the tenets of his moral sense, then, makes Roy feel at sea, and it is this sense of being adrift that his routinized compulsions attempt to correct for. Psychological and behavioral ballast to correct for moral tempests. The influence of Roy's moral compass is first displayed in his reluctance to instruct his spurious daughter in his craft and then in his insistence on her not profiting from the illustrative con into which he initiates her.

Because all of Roy's obsessive-compulsive anxiety and behaviors evaporate when he is forced out of the grifting life, we conclude that they were somehow debilitating repercussions of that life. Of course, most con men do not suffer as Roy does; however, we are prompted to wonder whether a career of tricking people out of their money may have other moral costs. As noted, in many of our films, con artists do not appear to have much of a social or personal life. Apart from their confederates, do grifters have room for real friends or family? One possible reason that they do not is the need to conceal their vocation from such individuals. A life built on deceiving people might then require so much further deception of those with whom we would be intimate that there is simply no "space" for such outside intimacy.

This would bear out the Socratic argument that the way we act toward others always has an impact on ourselves, not just on those we affect by our behavior. Indeed, following Socrates we might go further, in the following way. Because con artists are forever playing roles, concealing their true designs and motives from their marks, they must necessarily cut themselves off from portions of their own selves. Deceivers and manipulators are perforce put at a distance from dimensions of their own personalities or characters. If we take Roy to be an object lesson, an extreme example of his ilk, we can speculate that other con artists are, to a lesser extent, paying a steep price for their vocations. They just do not see it because the price is not as pronounced or as evident as Roy's more palpable, physical suffering. On this construal, the film becomes something of a cautionary morality tale. Here, there is a parallel with the lesson presented in *Groundhog Day* (Harold Ramis, 1993). People living ordinary lives cannot see how their selfish orientation keeps them from a truly happy life. Only when Phil is forced by the repetition Groundhog Day to confront the hollowness of his life does he see how the virtuous path is essential to happiness. As the only "victim" of the repetition, the one who realizes he is caught in the metaphysical cycle, Phil is uniquely positioned to

14   *Con Artist's Comeuppance and Cure:* Matchstick Men

learn from his plight, just as Roy is situated to learn from being his partner's prey. Other matchstick men would have to undergo a similar personal revelation in order to understand how robbing people through deceptive schemes actually works against their own true interests. As with Phil being bound to the same day in Groundhog Day, Roy's apparently devastating experience of being betrayed by his own partner is actually a blessing. Upending his career as a con man frees him to pursue an honest, and loving, life with an attractive woman. The pseudo-daughter who was part of Frank's long-con is ironically an image of what having a genuine family can mean.

The notion that Roy has a core of morality that is at odds with his grifting vocation invites inquiry into the moral character of con men in general and Roy in particular. First, we should note that certain virtues and vices simply come with the territory of the con game. Among the virtues necessary to success in flimflam are ingenuity, adaptability, and patience. Con artists must be ingenious in order to devise a narrative that will be plausible to potential marks and still facilitate relieving them of their money. Obviously, there is a continuum, with the best grifters being the most crafty. But con artists also need to be adaptable. Real events rarely unfold exactly as they have been scripted or envisioned. The behavior of would-be marks is likely to deviate from what is anticipated, and external events, often unforeseen, can interfere with plans; a car accident or bad weather, for example, can require that the con artist modifies his plan and behavior in order to reap his reward. Especially in long cons, the grifter must exercise patience. He must allow events and the mark's compliance to unfold in due course or the mark's suspicions may be aroused. Moreover, for most long cons to work, events and behavior must proceed in a series, earlier conditions enabling future situations to take place naturally, or seemingly naturally. Depending on the details of the con game and the gulls involved, other virtues may be required, such as courage (or its approximation) to face real danger or compassion (or its counterfeit) to resonate with another's suffering or hardship.

At the same time, various virtues are obviously ingredient in the con artist's chicanery. Dishonesty and deceit are the most blatant as they are built into the charade that frames the con game. But the con artist must also be impervious to the damage he is doing to the lives of the people he robs. Too much sensitivity to the harm he is causing is liable to weaken his resolve or undermine his acting performance. And, this is where Roy's tics and twitches come in. He is too attuned to the harm he is doing to escape with his marks' money unscathed. We might then attribute his own discomfort and disability to something like integrity, to the attack on it that he is himself waging.

Integrity characterizes an individual whose self is a coherent, consistent whole. Important aspects of the individual's personality reinforce one another rather than being disconnected or in conflict with one another. Gabriele Taylor and Raimond Gaita argue that the person with integrity is one "who keeps his self 'intact,' whose life is 'of a piece,' whose self is whole and integrated"

Con Artist's Comeuppance and Cure: Matchstick Men 15

(1981: 143). The person with integrity acts in ways that express his important values and commitments; someone who lacks integrity does not live up to his principles or what supposedly matters most to him. Integrity is maintained when the individual's everyday behavior keeps him intact, harmonizing the various aspects of his personality into a relatively integrated whole. Causing people loss and pain threatens Roy's deepest moral values and so puts him at odds with himself. The obsessive-compulsive antics are a vain attempt to compensate for the way his con games actually undermine his integrity. It is ironic that Roy may actually be hurting himself more than his victims through his success as a grifter.

Roy's integrity is in striking contrast to his partner's glaring vice: disloyalty. The reason we, in the audience, are so taken aback at the revelation of Frank's intricate con game is that we expect some form of loyalty to hold among partners in crime. The age-old double-cross seems more malevolent among con men than among other groups of criminals. The years of scheming and relying on one another, trusting one another to enact the script and improvise with guile when necessary, would seem to create a sturdier bond than in many other forms of larcenous cooperation. Frank's humor and seeming concern for Roy's mental health add to the stealth and cunning of his betrayal. It is one thing to take advantage of the weaknesses of strangers, but to trap Roy through a heartfelt relationship with a phony daughter seems to be the ultimate in disloyalty and callousness. When we learn at film's end that Frank has also cheated "Angela" after Roy's money has been taken in the denouement of the con, we realize the depths of Frank's disloyalty and utter lack of moral compunction. Truly, the antithesis of the morally plagued Roy.

The Story

When Frank comes over to rescue Roy (who has not been answering his phone), he sets Roy up with a shrink to provide therapy and medication. But this new therapist is really an actor and one good enough to fool both Roy and the audience. He is employed by Frank and everything that follows, we discover, is part of Frank's complex plan to steal his partner's pile of money from a well-secured bank account. That Frank has brought in an actor to play the role of therapist makes explicit the theatrical shape of his very clever and very protracted con. The next step is the ersatz therapist arranging for Roy to see the fourteen-year-old daughter Roy has supposedly sired, but never met, with his ex-wife. Planted by Frank, Angela is cute, spirited, and girlishly charming, although a good deal older than her advertised age. She soon insinuates herself into Roy's life. Showing up at his house, Angela claims to have had a fight with her mother and wants to camp out with Roy. She will later explain that it was because her mother refused to discuss Roy with her. Angela quotes her mother as saying that Roy was "a bad guy," Angela continues, "[but] you don't seem like a bad guy." Roy replies, "That's what makes me good at it."

16 *Con Artist's Comeuppance and Cure:* Matchstick Men

After Roy leaves his home for work, we see Angela listen to records, poke around Roy's digs, and discover a pistol and stash in a porcelain bulldog. She seems to be a genuinely curious teenager.

Overcoming his standard reluctance to buy into long cons, Roy has agreed to Frank's plan to steal from a man named Frechette. The deception involves a discrepancy in the currencies of Britain and the United States, and a nimble, surreptitious switching of briefcases in an airport. This turns out to be the hub of Frank's underlying trickery (and theft) of Roy, in which Angela will play an important part. Before the currency and briefcase swap, and its aftermath of staged violence, Roy gets to know and enjoy being with Angela. Despite her completely fabricated role in his life, she enriches it. We see him genuinely smile and laugh with her as she gobbles pizza and ice cream, argues with Roy, probes his life, giggles, and cries. Angela even plays a positive role in Roy's interactions with an attractive grocery store clerk. During several trips to the grocery store, Roy becomes more familiar with the friendly woman who seems to reciprocate his interest in her. Angela is part of this incipient relationship. When buying Angela's ice cream, for instance, he tells the clerk that it is not for him. He then chortles when she asks whether he has kids overnight. During another trip, Roy makes eye contact with the pretty woman and nods as she notices Angela with him. Interacting for the last time, the clerk asks after Roy's "cute little girl," remarking, "it must be lonesome without her." Turning to leave, Roy asks the woman, "It's Kathy, right?" and then introduces himself. The suggestion is that Roy's relationship with Angela is opening him up socially. When he later forgets to remove his shoes upon entering his home, we wonder whether she might also be freeing him a little from his compulsive routines.

Two pivotal scenes connect Roy more intimately with his newly discovered daughter. The first is an argument that we later suspect Angela of precipitating. The second is a lesson Roy delivers in playing a mark. Angela has gone out at night and Roy nervously waits up for her to come home. When she arrives stealthily through the patio doors, Roy demands to know where she has been and accuses her of "sneaking back in." Roy complains that Angela is throwing off the order in his life. Angela protests, saying that she did not even take money "from your stupid dog." Roy is taken aback by Angela's knowledge of the hiding place and, scolding her, scurries over to check the contents of his porcelain money and gun storage decoy: disguised as a knick-knack much as con men assume the guise of something or someone innocuous.

Angela starts to leave in a huff. Roy runs after her, calling her "sweetheart" and saying that he was not kicking her out. Angela wails that Roy cannot even tell her what he does for a living, sarcastically remarking that "Antique dealers [Roy's cover] always keep stacks of cash in their homes next to their guns." She so manipulates the scene that Roy winds up apologizing. He pleads that he is not very good at being a father and humorously, but poignantly, adds, "I barely get by being me." Totally capitulating, Roy asks Angela to come

Con Artist's Comeuppance and Cure: Matchstick Men   17

back inside his home, offers another pizza, and extends her stay with him to a whole week. Angela feigns incredulity when Roy discloses his true line of work and corrects her characterization, replacing "con man" with "con artist." Playing the intrigued little girl, Angela implores dad to teach her something.

Roy caves into Angela's demand that he teach her con games in the face of her threatening to tell him things she has done with boys that compromise her innocence. Nervously waiting up for his daughter to return home; wanting to spare her the sordidness of his work; wishing to maintain an idealized image of Angela as a sweet young thing: Angela's performance is transforming Roy into a fledgling father. At first, Roy declines to instruct her in the ways of the con artist because she is a "bright, beautiful, innocent girl" and he does not want to screw that up. In the process of teaching Angela about his craft, Roy also displays his basic moral decency. In words and deeds, he tries to impart moral truths. These efforts at cushioning Angela from the harms of being a matchstick man are added evidence of Roy's moral values and how they conflict with being a grifter. Before beginning his lesson, Roy confesses to Angela that he regrets that he steals from people "who don't deserve it; old people, fat people, lonely." He does not answer when Angela asks, "Then why do you do it?" just as he did not answer the "therapist" when he asked what Roy would do for a living if he did not cheat people out of their money. Roy's silences and expression of regret point to his vocation as the basis of his psychological handicaps. Obsessive-compulsive rituals, such as counting the same number upon entering or leaving his home, apparently provide Roy with a sense of control his gamesmanship undermines. Although he is in obvious control as a con artist, manipulating and robbing his marks, the work violates Roy's deeply held moral convictions. The result of this conflict is Roy feeling compromised, his life lacking in genuine (moral) order. To regain a semblance of control over his affairs, then, Roy unwittingly resorts to his compulsive rituals.

With the evening argument and Roy's disclosure of his racket to Angela, the scene is set for father's tutorial. He also instructs us, in the audience, about the parameters that make for successful flimflam. Roy's point of view dominates the film, including the revelation that he has been played for a sucker, and we experience events in the film from his perspective. However, the film dexterously repositions us as recipients of his pedagogy, as if occupying Angela's space, and this adds to the complexity of our experience of the story. Roy imparts rule number one: don't work near where you live, stipulating where the staging of the play should take place. Roy buys a lottery ticket, changes one number on it, and tells Angela that the most important thing about the game he is teaching her is that it is 90% variable. Because unforeseen things happen, you "gotta be flexible." Grifters clearly delight in their ability to build a script but improvise when circumstances demand it. We also see that dupes tend not to be totally innocent, as the opportunity for found money makes them susceptible to the con. Roy wrinkles the lottery ticket and alters it, preparing the prop for the ensuing mini-drama.

18 *Con Artist's Comeuppance and Cure:* Matchstick Men

In a laundromat, Angela chats with an older female patron and drops the ticket on the floor; pretending to discover the ticket, she notes that "It's not mine." She and the woman compare it with the winning number found in the newspaper the seated Roy supplies; Roy is playing the low-key part of the helpful stranger. The woman makes a call ascertaining that they've won a nice secondary amount with a ticket that sports four of the requisite five digits and secures Angela's share from an ATM machine (because the girl cannot accompany her to collect). When the woman eventually realizes that the ticket has been altered, therefore, she will be out the money she has fronted to Angela. Roy compliments Angela as she gets in the car, but insists she return the stolen money, claiming that it is his duty as a responsible father not to allow his daughter to steal. All the while, of course, Roy's growing entwinement with Angela is integral to his being robbed blind. He enthusiastically recounts the incident with his therapist, exclaiming how excited he is to have a daughter, adding, "And I'm not scared shitless." As a result of their argument and the successful collaborative ruse, Roy is indeed developing a paternal relationship for the first time in his life. Taking his responsibilities as a father seriously is facilitated by Angela's winsome ways and the pleasure Roy takes in being with her. He will later tell his partner, Frank, that he has to stop the con life. Roy's experience of a "straight" life is so invigorating and fulfilling that he decides to relinquish the lucrative and entertaining rewards of being a con artist even before he is made the victim of his own vocation.

Frank's Masterful Con Revealed

The scam of Frechette in the airport involves Angela distracting the would-be mark so Roy can switch briefcases, thereby heisting Frechette's money. Like the doctored lottery ticket, the briefcase is the prop upon which the entire ploy turns. The con goes sideways as Frechette comes running after Roy and Angela in the airport parking ramp. Roy is soon chagrined to return home to find an apparently battered Frank and an armed Frechette. The erstwhile mark claims to have traced Angela through airport security cameras and police records (which allegedly indicate that Angela has a police record) and threatens legal proceedings against her unless he is given more money. Going to retrieve the money from the porcelain dog, Angela instead apparently shoots Frechette with the hidden pistol. Here, the movie conforms to the genre's use of the ruse of violence to pull off the con: first with the apparent battering of Frank, now with the sham shooting of Frechette. Holding the sobbing girl, Roy tells her that he will say he did the shooting. The pretend violence, done to Frank and Frechette, is now followed by Frechette delivering real blows that render Roy unconscious. In this respect, *Matchstick Men* deviates from the avoidance of violence in con artist films, and this compounds its norm-breaking by having the con game played on a practitioner of the art.

What is the significance of including actual violence in the perpetration of the grift? For one thing, the absence of real violence is shown to be, itself, a

Con Artist's Comeuppance and Cure: Matchstick Men   19

sop, barely veiling the seriousness of the crime. The individuals who are the gulls are violated by the scam and theft just as surely as if they had been physically abused. As John will say in *Birthday Girl*, their dignity is trampled along with their pocketbooks being emptied. Second, the violence done to Roy indicates that con artists are not above doing physical harm if it is necessary for the success of their scheme. True, conning someone out of his money without inflicting physical damage is more elegant, but such brutality is not automatically precluded by the grift. Lastly, the film indicates that actual violence from legal authorities or a mark who gets wise to the game is an ever-present danger. The con artist is always at risk of being caught and punished, sometimes officially, sometimes informally. A con man does, in fact, suffer at the hands of a would-be gull in Stephen Frears's film *The Grifters* (1990).

Recovering in a phony hospital room, Roy is guarded by fake policemen who inform him that Frechette is dead and that the prints on the gun are too small to be his; Angela therefore appears to Roy to be in serious trouble. He asks to see his shrink to whom he gives his precious bank passcode so that Angela can escape with his accumulated boodle. The threat to Angela, then, serves as the fulcrum to lure Roy into divulging the secret key to his horde of (swindled) money. Roy soon reads an explanatory letter from Frank, the therapist's office is abandoned, and his former wife tells him that the baby she had been carrying had died. Frank's cast of characters includes the therapist, Angela, Frechette, and the police. But Frank was also playing a part: the somewhat goofy, cowboy-hat-wearing, sentimental sidekick who tells Roy that he loves him. Like an epilogue, we see Roy selling low-end carpet a year later. Angela and her boyfriend come into the store and she apologizes for ripping him off, confiding that, after all, Frank cheated her out of her share of the con. Like a father, Roy criticizes her alluring attire but agrees that they did have a good time together. He philosophically notes that she did not take his money, "I gave it to you." Angela playfully bids him goodbye with, "I'll see you dad," not quite realizing that she did after all help make him a father.

By trapping Roy through his con and stripping him of his larcenous winnings, Frank has inadvertently freed his former partner from the criminal life and the toll it had taken on his psyche. The salutary upshot of Roy's loss of economic fortune might put us in mind of the allegorical cast of Silas Marner's story.[5] In both cases, individuals preoccupied with money are cleaned out and, in its stead, enjoy the bounty of the human companionship and love of which they formerly had been deprived. By injecting Angela into Roy's life, Frank has also enabled Roy to care enough about somebody else to subordinate his own interests to her welfare. Although Angela was playing a role, its effects on Roy are real and lasting. He has made a new, more pedestrian home with the comely grocery clerk and she is expecting their baby. The impostor offspring has unwittingly helped engender a genuine child for Roy.

For Roy, the matchstick man, being the victim of the scheme, has freed him from a desolate life filled with obsessive-compulsive tics and twitches. Roy's affection and care for his phony daughter begin the process of uprooting

20   *Con Artist's Comeuppance and Cure:* Matchstick Men

him from the isolation of the life of the con artist. For Roy, the connection with Angela is real and he begins to envision a way of life on the up and up. When he is finally tricked out of almost all his savings, Roy is ready to live the more ordinary, but less conflicted, life of a working stiff. He has settled down with the pretty grocery store clerk, prepared to be the father of a child that is genuinely his own. The moral of Roy's story, then, is that habitually pretending to be something and someone you are not does distance you from who you really are or can be. Ensnaring unsuspecting people by camouflaging ourselves blocks us from our true, moral natures. Roy feels this distance as a lack of control and so needs to be obsessively clean and tidy, repeating incantations that keep his anxiety barely at bay.

Notes

1 *Nine Queens* and *Ladies vs. Ricky Bahl* also show grifters being conned; however, the former concludes with a more complete vanquishing of the con man.
2 A short con, as its name implies, is pulled off in a relatively brief period of time, limiting the con man's exposure to detection or risk. In contrast, a long con can take days or weeks to unspool, as in the scenarios created to cheat Roy and Margaret in our first two film stories. Compensating for the increased danger of the long con, however, is the prospect of a bigger payday.
3 This is also evident, for instance, in the arid life of the psychologist Margaret in our next film *House of Games* (David Mamet, 1987) and the lonely lives (separately) led by both Roy and his mother, Lily, in Stephen Frears' *The Grifters* (1990).
4 The illusion of violence is also at work in the cons of *The Sting, The Last Seduction,* and *Gone Girl*; whereas, all too real violence marks several incidents in *The Grifters*, especially its grisly finale.
5 In George Eliot's tale, Silas is a miserly recluse whose hoard of gold is stolen but is providentially replaced by a foundling baby girl whose golden locks resemble it. The monetary treasure seems to Silas converted into a precious, living gift, something the loveless Silas needs far more than a store of coins.

Bibliography

Taylor, Gabriele and Raymond Gaita (1981). "Integrity." *Proceedings of the Aristotelian Society*, Supp. 1, 143–159.

Filmography

Bielinsky, Fabian (2000). *Nine Queens.* Argentina.
Dahl, John (1994). *The Last Seduction.* U.S.
Fincher (2014). *Gone Girl.* U.S.
Frears, Stephen (1990). *The Grifters.* U.S.
Hill, George Roy (1973). *The Sting.* U.S.
Mamet, David (1987). *House of Games.* U.S.
Ramis, Harold (1993). *Groundhog Day.* U.S.
Scott, Ridley (2003). *Matchstick Men.* U.S.
Sharma, Maneesh (2011). *Ladies vs. Ricky Bahl.* India.

2 Revenge and Self-Knowledge

House of Games

Parallel Dupes

I will begin discussing *House of Games* by connecting it with our previous film, *Matchstick Men*. In both films, the protagonists' original situation and psychology undergo a radical alteration as a result of a life-changing con played on them. The stories of Roy Waller and Margaret Ford follow a similar trajectory, but with drastically different outcomes. At first, these main characters seem to have little in common. Roy is a successful con artist, typically working short cons with his partner, Frank. Margaret Ford is a well-regarded psychologist who has recently made a splash with her book, *Driven*, dealing with compulsive behavior. If anything, then, Roy would seem to be a likely candidate to be one of Margaret's patients, plagued as he is with a variety of tics and obsessive-compulsive actions. And we do see her working carefully and thoughtfully with several of her patients. Unlike Roy, Margaret is calm and is not easily rattled when unanticipated events come her way. Then, too, Margaret's is a legitimate, respected profession whose aim is to help people; whereas Roy's work is criminal and designed to hurt people.

Yet, similarities between the lives of the protagonists of our two films, and not just in their film stories, soon begin to emerge. Roy and Margaret both live in comfortable homes, but their domiciles are bland, bordering on the sterile. The lack of individuality and vitality in their homes presents an environmental image of the emptiness of their interpersonal lives. Neither have real friends. Roy has his grifting sidekick, Frank, and Margaret has her mentor, the older psychologist, Dr. Littauer. But both are professional relationships injected with a bit of camaraderie. In addition, both characters seem consumed by their work; neither individual does anything outside conning or ministering to people. In other words, the lives of Roy and Margaret are desolate, until, that is, they are ensnared in the schemes of creative con men. As their lives become more fulfilling socially, moreover, their stories follow parallel arcs.

Most blatant is the fact that both are the marks of elaborate and extended ("long") con games played by people they know to be hustlers yet do not suspect. Both swindles, moreover, are set in motion by the protagonist entering

DOI: 10.4324/9781003364542-3

22   *Revenge and Self-Knowledge:* House of Games

into a new heterosexual relationship: Roy with his alleged daughter, Angela; Margaret with the slick grifter Mike – who hangs out at the club, The House of Games. For Roy and Margaret, these newfound relationships add appreciably to their lackluster social lives, even as they serve to embroil the protagonists in the fraudulent webs that will cost them dearly. As indicated, we, in the audience, are also drawn into the ruses with Roy and Margaret, so that we realize they have been conned along with them, at the exact same moment. Each of the schemes turns on spurious legal risk and each yields huge monetary gains for the masterminding con artists. Yet, after they discover the trickery that bilks them out of heaps of cash, both characters manage to get on with their lives, better for the seemingly devastating experience. Although both of their lives improve, they do so in a morally divergent fashion. Roy settles down to a drab, but satisfying life, while Margaret begins to walk on the dark side.[1]

Two other shared ingredients link the stories of Roy and Margaret losing money to an ingenious grifter. Both tales include explicit instruction in the art of conning as well as carefully orchestrated violence. As we saw in the previous chapter, Roy provides valuable instruction to his purported daughter, Angela, imparting such gems as not working the con near home and being ready to improvise. Having the person who is the ultimate gull offer a tutorial in conning adds a layer of irony to a story rich in ironies; for example, Roy's loss of his larcenous money enriches him. *House of Games* is more straightforward. Margaret is taught various con artist tricks by the hucksters. Part of the attraction of the ploys and charades, no doubt, lies in the psychology that informs the subterfuge. As she herself notes, Margaret has a professional interest in how the grifters exploit the attitudes and thoughts of ordinary people. But we wonder if there is more to it. By the story's end, we wonder whether exposure to the House of Games crew taking advantage of people's weaknesses in immoral and illegal ways appeals to Margaret's dormant proclivities.

In both films, the illusion of violence is the fulcrum on which the flimflam turns. In *House of Games*, an intentionally clumsy instance of a staged threat of gun use is followed by the well-scripted, plausible phony violence that the con men use to relieve Margaret of her sizable savings. Yet, these pretenses surprisingly foreshadow actual killing at the story's denouement. As noted in the previous chapter, the movies invite reflection on the relationship between violence and stealing through con games. Many con games employ the appearance of violence or allusions to it. However, the pretense of physical harm that often shapes the games con men play seems a shadow of the genuine danger potentially in store for the grifters as well as their marks. Just how close do the con games come to giving way to serious injury or death? Moreover, there is a strong affinity between the violent and nonviolent methods employed by killers and con men, respectively. Where actual violence is blatant in its trampling of personal volition and well-being, the con game is no less a violation of personhood, despite its veneer of soft trickery.

Revenge and Self-Knowledge: House of Games   23

As a result of discovering that she has been the target of an elaborate grift, Margaret retaliates. In so doing, she discovers depths of her own criminal nature that had been hidden or, more likely, repressed. Its subterranean gravity may be the reason she is drawn to studying the con artists in the first place. But her revenge is not simply for the theft of a sizable chunk of her bank account. It is also for being taken in by an erotic relationship that she believed was real. In fact, the sexual deception may be more painful than the loss of money, but whichever predominates, Margaret is stung by being played for a patsy, in larceny and love. She seeks revenge out of the feeling of humiliation. This is the moral force that propels Margaret into killing and this act, in turn, "liberates" her to further criminality.

To get clear on humiliation, we need to compare it with its cognate, humility. On the surface, humiliation and humility are alike. Simone Weil writes that "there is a resemblance between the lower and the higher. Hence... humiliation is an image of humility" (1977: 352). When someone is humiliated or humbled, their self-regard is deflated as a result of an unanticipated, untoward experience. Humiliating and humbling incidents both tend to produce psychological dislocation or discomfort as a result of an exposure to a flaw or inadequacy in the exposed individual. And the same experience could deepen one person's humility while causing another individual to feel humiliated. However, being humbled and being humiliated differ with regard to self-understanding and diverge dramatically in the relationship the individual has with herself and with other people.

The humiliated individual typically becomes angry over her self-exposure. The person feels foolish but is also irate. At first blush, the anger appears directed at herself, for her failure to perform as expected or desired: flubbing a play in a sport, missing a crucial aspect of a report, and being caught in a lie. Yet, the humiliation also seems to include other people, in particular, their viewing of her flaws or failure. We can ask whether an individual would feel humiliated without her deflating moment being witnessed by other people or being imagined as being so witnessed. Humiliated individuals are often angry at others, secretly blaming them or circumstances for their own degradation being on view. The upshot may well be that humiliation leaves the individual simply wishing that events had not conspired against her or that she had been spared the misfortune of being brought low.

The alteration that accompanies humiliation is typically only partial and superficial. The individual resolves to avoid letting herself be put in jeopardy. The humiliated individual is reminded of her precarious place in the world or of her dependence on the fickle opinion of others. Her self-evaluation is forced downward and she chafes at her lack of independence. Humiliation motivates the individual to protect herself from looking bad.

The moral perspective that undergirds humility has two fundamental dimensions: a moral standard or ideal and our radical dependence. We can maintain our humility by gauging ourselves by an independent, supreme

24 *Revenge and Self-Knowledge:* House of Games

ideal. For some, this is God's perfection or the perfection to which He bids us aspire. Of course, we can also compare our moral character to that of other people (such as saints), but such a self-assessment is really but a step on the way to the full ideal, or an approximation of it. Obviously, the moral standard need not refer to a divine being, as Aristotle's view of the virtuous individual demonstrates. Whether religious or secular, the idea is that individuals govern their self-assessment by moral values that are objective, general, and action-guiding. Doing so, I argue, enables even people of outstanding technical or moral achievement to remain humble.

The moral viewpoint also includes acknowledging our radical dependence on forces that promote our ability and success. Religious people are ever mindful of their dependence on God for their natural ability and for the discipline needed to develop it. Secular individuals can maintain an awareness of their dependence on the fortuitous influences in their lives, sensitive to the fact that with a twist of fate, or DNA, they would not have the talent or achievement they do. However much we accomplish, it depends to a great extent on our genetic endowment, parental nurture, education, and just plain luck to have the necessary opportunities to shine. Radical dependence is moral because it involves appreciating that we are not responsible for the varied aspects of life on which our advantages and success hinge; therefore, they are not deserved.

Built on this moral perspective, the humble person has a realistic view of his strengths and weaknesses, neither overestimating his true value nor selling it short. As such, humility does indeed occupy the Aristotelian mean between the vicious extremes of arrogance (or excessive pride) and self-denigration. Moreover, when he achieves something worthwhile, humility informs the individual's acknowledgment of the people and opportunities that make it possible. Gratitude for these advantages necessarily follows the pull of humility. With a foundation of humility, then, an individual takes his humbling experience in stride, even feeling gratitude for seeing afresh his limitations and adjusting appropriately to his self-estimation. We can now see that when an individual is humiliated rather than humbled by a failure, it is likely due to an underlying failure of humility itself. The experience of humiliation, I suggest, is plausibly viewed as conditioned by the individual's arrogance. Arrogance involves a mistaken, excessive estimation of our worth, either in general or with regard to a particular ability, such as in athletics, science, or medicine. Therefore, the humility that is informed by the moral perspective not only keeps our success in proper perspective but also keeps the lack of achievement from flattening us with humiliation.

In contrast with the humiliated person, the humbled individual sees himself more clearly and experiences the disappointing moment as self-edifying. A humbling experience turns us inward. We can be humbled, but not humiliated, without other people being aware of our failing. When humbled by circumstance or by our own behavior, we gain in self-understanding and fittingly lower our self-assessment. The increase in humility gained by this

Revenge and Self-Knowledge: House of Games   25

reassessment requires that we be open to recognizing our flaws. And this openness is supplied by the humility that already exists. When humbled, we are grateful for the correction of error in judgment about ourselves. This is why Nancy Snow observes that "humbling experiences...are parts of the educative process of personal growth, maturation, and ongoing development. We learn our limits through humbling experiences" (1995: 214). However, without an existing stratum of humility to begin with, we would be unable to appreciate the real meaning of the deflating experience and this is what happens in humiliation. The humble person has the requisite self-knowledge and perspective to be open to correction. When people are humiliated, they have failed beforehand to situate their superiority in the moral perspective that governs humility in its fullest expression.

When Margaret is humiliated by discovering, in one fell swoop, that she has been conned out of her money and sexually manipulated, her preexisting arrogance has disposed her to this reaction. Notice how this contrasts with Roy's response to learning that his long-time partner in crime has so adroitly pulled the wool over his very expert con man eyes. Roy accepts his failure, indicating that along with the moral core that causes his distressed compulsions while plying his deceitful trade, he is not after all, an arrogant man. As with a genuinely humble individual, Roy learns from his comeuppance: he gives up the grifter's life and settles down to a hum-drum, but tic-free domestic life, replete with a winsome wife and baby on the way. Margaret, however, must salve her wounded pride. Of course, Mike, the con artist, is hardly an innocent. But his grift does not seem quite severe enough to warrant a death sentence. Only in light of Margaret's pride-fueled humiliation can we make sense of his demise at her hands. But that is half the startling conclusion and before it arrives, the film takes us on an instructive journey into the world of con games, replete with explicit instruction.

The Mark Strikes Back

House of Games has a sturdy structure. It opens and closes with its protagonist, Margaret Ford (Lindsay Crouse), being asked to sign her newly published book by a grateful reader as she accompanies her former teacher in a well-appointed restaurant (yet, never partaking of a meal). In the opening scene, Dr. Wittauer (Lilla Skala) counsels Margaret not to work so hard and to find more enjoyment in life. In the closing scene, the mentor acknowledges that Margaret's been away, apparently on vacation, and so has taken her earlier advice. As part of enjoying life more fully, the older therapist had also encouraged Margaret to buy herself a beautiful gold cigarette lighter, like the one she had been admiring earlier. Instead, Margaret ends the film by swiping such a lighter from a neighboring woman's handbag in the restaurant. Moreover, in place of her usual stylish but sedate attire of muted beige or gray, Margaret is now dressed in a colorful, tropical dress. What has transpired

26 *Revenge and Self-Knowledge:* House of Games

between the beginning and closing scenes explains Margaret's newfound bold thieving and flair for life.

The intricate con into which Margaret is drawn begins with a planted patient. Billy Hahn is cast as a compulsive gambler who brandishes a gun with which he threatens to kill himself. He claims to owe 25,000 dollars to an "unbeatable gambler:" Mike (Joe Mantegna), a con artist at the club The House of Games. Billy's stint as Margaret's patient is the first of four carefully contrived scenes staged by Mike to set Margaret up for the grand scam that will extract the hefty savings from her bank account. Promising to help Billy with his problem in exchange for the gun, Margaret goes to the club and confronts Mike over the debt. The shadows and old-fashioned dialogue give the film a throwback, noirish feel. For example, Mike calls Margaret "a caution," and she tells him she wants to "talk turkey." But it turns out that Billy's IOU is just for $800 and the film leaves two questions unanswered. Why did Billy exaggerate exponentially and why is Margaret not perplexed or at least curious about the hyperbole? Be that as it may, she is soon instructed in the nature of a "tell." She will also learn of the "flue:" a simple trick for stealing the money that the grifter merely appears to be sliding into an envelope.

A "tell," she learns, is a non-verbal way of unintentionally conveying information: "telling" a person something that you do not want them to know. In exchange for Billy's debt, Margaret agrees to communicate a particular gambler's bluffing tell to Mike, who is going to leave the poker game that is taking place in the next room. Their brief partnership is soon revealed as a ruse to bilk Margaret out of a tidy sum ($6,000); however, "accidentally" exposing the attempt to con her is intentional, itself part of the encompassing plan to inveigle a much larger sum from her.[2] Like Margaret, however, we, in the audience, take events at their face value, accepting that Billy Hahn is a compulsive gambler who owes money and the "gaff" (trick) in the gambling scene was actually "blown" (botched). But these episodes are merely designed to entice Margaret and she does indeed accept Mike's parting invitation to return when she would "enjoy some more excitement." We then see him standing in the middle of the road watching her pull away in a cab, impossibly in shadows, compounding the stylized presentation.

When Margaret joins her mentor for the second time in a restaurant, she aligns herself with the con men. Lamenting her inability to help a girl in prison and other patients avoid their mistakes, Margaret echoes Billy's previous accusation, claiming about her professional work, "it's a sham, a con game." She feels that she is deceiving people because she cannot really help them. Perhaps Margaret is prompted to seek out Mike again by her former teacher's admonition to find some enjoyment outside work. Although she tells Mike she wants to do a study of con men, Margaret seems more interested in the gamesmanship involved than in doing genuine research for another book. He takes her to a Western Union office for further education in the arts of the flimflam. First, he explains that the confidence in question is not the obvious

Revenge and Self-Knowledge: House of Games   27

trust the mark gives the trickster. Rather, the confidence that is the leverage for the ploy is actually bestowed by the con man on the victim. Since this is a pretense, part of the con man's act, the dissembling of bestowing his faith in the victim lays the groundwork for the transactional deception that finally yields the theft of the mark's money: deception thereby compounds deception.

To illustrate his lesson, Mike pursues a recent arrival at the Western Union, but this would be chump (we later discover) is also a member of Mike's thieving troupe, playing the character of a Sergeant Moran (William Macy) in the third scene of the grand charade that targets Margaret's savings. By offering to lend the military man the money he needs before the arrival of his own anticipated wired funds, Mike demonstrates how the con man demonstrates confidence in the integrity of the potential victim. He tells Margaret, "Now that man is going to give his money to a total stranger [himself]," but eventually refuses the spurious mark's offer of cash. In front of Margaret, Mike takes the high road of declining the rewards of the grift, much as Roy had done with Angela's windfall in the laundromat scam. Mike chortles, "What's more fun than human nature?" He is inviting Margaret to see the joy in playing the con game. As noted, the con artist and we, in the audience, delight not just in the stolen money, but in the ingenuity of the con and the suspense of seeing whether it will work. Yet here, the brief game and its enjoyment are framed by the larger theatrical production of which Margaret is ignorant.

Mike soon asks Margaret if she wants to make love, saying that we cannot hide the things we think and want. Mike says that Margaret wants someone to come along, possess her, and take her "into a new thing." She acknowledges the truth of this and accompanies her new teacher into a fashionable hotel for the fourth dramatic episode preparatory to the major coup. Billy Hahn's compulsive gambling led to the intentionally bungled gambling con, which was followed by the Western Union demonstration. Now, Mike snatches the key left by a tuxedoed gent on the hotel desk so he and Margaret can have a sexual tryst in the man's room. The thrill of "stealing" the room adds to the naughtiness of the improvised romantic encounter for Margaret, unaware as she is that the man in the tuxedo is another of Mike's confederates. After they make love, Margaret pockets a penknife sitting on the bureau. This will prove important to the climax of her relationship with Mike and also as an indication of Margaret's suppressed inclinations.

Upon exiting the hotel, Mike tells Margaret that there is a "bit" (a trick that is part of a con job) he is supposed to do in front of the hotel with his partner Joey (Mike Nussbaum) who is walking down the street in the company of another, unfamiliar man. This apparent stranger, someone Joey has purportedly met at a conference or convention, is going to be set up as the alleged patsy of the embedded con that is actually designed to fleece Margaret. He will play a role analogous to the part Frechette played in *Matchstick Men*: that of the purported sucker who is actually in cahoots with the con men Margaret knows. As with Angela, Margaret implores Mike to include her in

28 *Revenge and Self-Knowledge:* House of Games

the impending scheme. Although Angela was in on the trickery of Roy and Margaret is the dupe, both genuinely delight in the artistry of the con. The play-acting according to a devious script that nevertheless demands improvisation speaks to a creative, venturous dimension of this brand of thievery that motivates its perpetrators in addition to the pecuniary payoff. Mike facetiously warns Margaret that the planned scam is not a game, but, of course, it is and it is to be played on the now romantically entangled psychologist. When another member of the gang inadvertently forgets his briefcase on the curb before taking off in a cab, Mike and Margaret stand with Joey and his new acquaintance gazing at the briefcase. As we would expect, it is loaded with cash which is the subject of ongoing discussion, into the night, in the room of a nearby hotel.

The apparent grift aims to defraud the stranger who accompanies Joey, but Margaret overhears him on a walkie-talkie in the bathroom, quietly making arrangements to arrest the larcenous trio, and also glimpses his gun. She tells Mike and Joey that the man is a cop. After a struggle, the con man posing as a cop appears to be shot and killed (again, just as Frechette was apparently shot by Angela). Mike and Joey flee the hotel in a car that Margaret steals and drives out of the garage, but Joey has (conveniently) forgotten the briefcase. Mike claims that it contains 80,000 dollars that the cronies have borrowed from mobsters for their con; ergo, they need Margaret to replace the "lost" money, and she does. She may be feeling guilty for the foiled caper as Joey had been criticizing Mike for bringing her along, for having confidence in her, and blames her for the (phony) policeman's death.

Mike tells Margaret that he and Joey are going away for a while because of the dead "cop," but that she can stay since no one knows her. He tells her to resist the urge to confess to the theft and murder because it was an accident. Back in her office, Margaret tears her diploma off the wall and removes her blouse, bloodied from the fake shooting. When Billy Hahn shows up at her office to tell her that he is cancelling his next appointment, a distraught Margaret suggests suspending treatment altogether. On her way to a dumpster to throw out the soiled blouse, she notices Billy at a pay phone. When she sees him get into the same red convertible that she thought she was stealing from the hotel's garage, she smells a rat. Now, wearing a hooded sweatshirt instead of her usual tailored attire, she spots the sporty car outside the bar at which she had met with Mike a second time. Margaret slips into the building through the rear entrance and spies on the whole coterie of confederates, including the men who played the tuxedoed hotel guest and the shot cop. She hears Mike talking about her stealing his penknife at the hotel and referring to sex with her as "a small price to pay" – adding (personal) insult to (monetary) injury. Margaret looks devastated and despondent. Being romantically manipulated adds personal insult to the financial injury of losing her loot.

At the airport where Mike is heading for Las Vegas, Margaret hurries over to him feigning fear of the police. She acts clingy and tells Mike that

Revenge and Self-Knowledge: House of Games   29

they can leave together as she took all of her money out of the bank and gives him the key to a locker where a quarter of a million dollars is supposed to be stashed. In a secluded area of the airport, Mike puts his arm around Margaret and comforts her. She protests that she knows she's bad and confesses to taking his penknife at the hotel. But she has given herself away as wise to Mike because she should not have known it was *his* knife rather than one belonging to the room's occupant (the tuxedoed gentleman). She only knows the penknife belongs to Mike because she has overheard him talking to his gang of con artists in the bar. Mike immediately grasps her slip and chides her for revealing that she knows she has been tricked and can no longer play the role of the frightened, and ignorant, accomplice. We do not know what Margaret was planning to do with or to Mike had she not blown her own little gaff. Instead, like a good grifter, she improvises by pulling out Billy's gun and ordering Mike to sit down. He defies her threat to kill him and Margaret coolly replies, "What is life without adventure." Margaret is clearly reveling in being in the driver's seat and Mike is now not so sure about her.

Margaret accuses Mike of using her and raping her – loosely understood as taking her sexually under false pretenses. Mike rejoins that she has learned some things about herself that she would rather not know. And this is soon shown in the film to be quite accurate. Unfortunately for Mike, he has correctly assessed Margaret's unrealized darker "drives." Margaret learns that she is capable of revenge and theft, besides the casual sex and participation in the ersatz con game. When Mike gets up and scoffs that she is bluffing in her threat of violence, Margaret shoots him in the leg. Mike bellows, "Are you nuts?" In his view, suckering someone in a con game does not merit shooting and he disavows ever being violent himself. But he has underestimated Margaret on two scores. First, her vanity or pride has been severely wounded; she has been humiliated by both the theft through deception and by the dismissal of their romantic connection as part of the ploy. She therefore demands that Mike beg for his life to restore her self-esteem by making him grovel. Mike repeats his belief that Margaret is bluffing, asking whether she is going to give up all the good things in her life just to kill him. Margaret calmly points out, "It's not my pistol. I was never here;" and commands him, "Beg for your life or I'm going to kill you." She tells Mike that she is out of control, but her demeanor indicates that she is very much in control. Mike defies her, and Margaret shoots him several times, as she replaces the gun in her handbag and leaves Mike for dead. Walking away from the screened-off area, Margaret is framed in shadow, reversing the earlier, shrouded shot of Mike in the middle of the street looking after Margaret pulling away in a taxi. The shadiness of Mike's dealing, it is suggested, has now been transferred to Margaret who will soon augment murder with stealthy theft.

***

30   *Revenge and Self-Knowledge:* House of Games

The violence that is often performed for effect in con games and that sometimes seems to percolate beneath their veneer of trickery has now surfaced and in the most unlikely of ways. A respected, published psychologist has violently dispatched a would-be lover for demeaning her by cheating her out of money and discounting her as an erotic partner. Mike's refusal to placate Margaret by pleading for her not to kill him elicits from her the murderous force that perhaps truly animates the con artist. Indeed, both Joey and Mike have used the metaphor of "killing," in the service of the big con, for being financially destroyed. Several times Joey bemoaned Margaret "killing" them with her ineptitude and Mike has accused Joey of "murdering" them by forgetting the briefcase with the money in the garage. When we play a con game on someone, we do violence by other means; we violate them, not just in the sense of robbing them but also in the sense of using their credulity against them. We violate their humanity by manipulating their thought and emotion and, in the end, violating their trust. Of course, this does not justify killing the flimflam artist, but the sexual and emotional violation Margaret experiences somehow thumps a primitive nerve.

In the film's closing scene, Margaret is once again dining out with Dr. Littauer, her former teacher and encouraging mentor. Her tasteful, but subdued ensembles have given way to a gaily colored dress and Margaret is sipping a tropical drink. From the conversation, we infer that Margaret has been vacationing in a sunny clime and she is smiling more. As in the opening scene, she signs a fan's copy of her book. This time, she inscribes, "forgive yourself," passing on her mentor's earlier advice for what Margaret should do if she behaves in an unforgivable way. And yet, from the way Margaret comports herself and her subsequent behavior, it does not seem as though Margaret feels the need to forgive herself. She is certainly unrepentant when, instead of heeding the older woman's suggestion to purchase a luxurious cigarette lighter, Margaret smoothly lifts just such a golden trophy from the handbag of the woman at the next table. She immediately uses the stolen treasure to fire up her own cigarette. Margaret thereby confirms Mike's earlier claim to chums that she is a thief, a "booster." Having acted out what may well be her personal compulsion, what "drives" her, Margaret smiles contentedly to herself to end the film.

Both Margaret and Roy have been transformed through suffering the devastation of a master con job, albeit in opposite directions. For Roy, the matchstick man being the victim of the scheme has freed him from a desolate life filled with obsessive-compulsive tics, twitches, and compulsively repeated phrases. The clash of his con artistry with his moral principles has debilitated Roy. With what is left of his integrity in tatters, he is barely functional and terribly unhappy. Roy's lively and caring relationship with his manufactured daughter has begun to free him from the lonely and immoral life of clever thievery. For Roy, the relationship is real and with Angela he finds genuine emotion, including joy in life. When he is finally plundered

Revenge and Self-Knowledge: House of Games 31

of almost all his stolen booty, Roy is ready to live the more prosaic, but less compromised, life of a blue-collar worker. He has made a home with the attractive worker from the grocery store and is looking forward to being the father of a child who, this time, is truly his own. Roy has learned valuable truths about the good life and himself: that routinely playing devious roles in order to rob people sets him morally adrift, uncoupling him from his moral bearings. Roy's obsessive-compulsive behaviors are a flailing attempt to regain some order in his life: the physical patterns and fastidiousness compensate for the moral disorder brought about through swindling people. Unlike Margaret, Roy does not experience being the victim of the sort of con games upon which he has thrived as an assault on his pride. Instead, he has enough humility to understand it as the pivotal occasion for changing his life – morally, for the better.

Being the victim of a huge con has also liberated Margaret, but for larcenous activity. Where Roy has been dislodged from a vocation of cunning criminality, Margaret has been drawn into a sideline of violence and theft. The compulsion to take what she could easily pay for had been repressed until the fling with a clever grifter. The detached psychologist has been invigorated by her brush with flimflam. The excitement of which Mike spoke did indeed enliven her and evoke a daring of which she did not know she was capable. The spontaneous sex in an apparently usurped hotel room; the theft of its occupant's penknife; participating in the money-in-the-briefcase con; and then shooting Mike have freed Margaret to a novel perspective on risk-taking and transgression. Her climactic theft of the gold cigarette lighter mirrors the robbery that is the purpose of all con games, but without the play-acting and deception of the gaff. Even so, Margaret uses a small bit of trickery and deception to get the owner of the lighter to look away in the restaurant just long enough for her to filch the coveted object. Her vibrant clothing and tropical drink after a balmy vacation emblematize her sunnier outlook on life. The self-satisfied smile Margaret wears after pilfering her prize leaves us to wonder what her life will be like from now on. Clearly, not the staid domesticity we project for Roy.

Notes

1 Another cinematic example of an event that seems catastrophic for the protagonist but turns out to liberate him occurs in *Wonder Boys*. When English Professor Grady Tripp sees the novel he has been laboring on for years flap away into the air, he is crestfallen; however, losing the work that has mushroomed out of control to over 2,000 pages, actually frees him. It frees Grady from a series of self-destructive habits, into a loving relationship, and the writing of a luminous story: the one we have been watching on the screen.

2 The scene plays as farce as the gun used as a prop is clumsily revealed to be a water pistol when liquid leaks out onto the poker table. The gambler who had been threatening Mike with the pistol comically protests that he couldn't convincingly brandish a gun that was not "loaded."

32 *Revenge and Self-Knowledge:* House of Games

Bibliography

Snow, Nancy (1995). "Humility." *Journal of Value Inquiry,* 29, 203–216.
Weil, Simone (1977). *Simone Weil Reader*, Ed. George Panichas. Rhode Island: Moyer Bell Press.

Filmography

Kloves, Steve (2000). *Wonder Boys.* U.S.
Mamet, David (1987). *House of Games.* U.S.
Scott, Ridley (2003). *Matchstick Men.* U.S.

3 The Femme Fatale as Con Artist

Body Heat

Enriching a Bewitching Character-Type

The femme fatale has long been a staple of cinema, stretching back to such actresses as Theda Bara (in the silent era) and Marlene Dietrich in the early days of talkies. Their characters use their feminine charms and wiles to manipulate men in pursuit of various aims. In her movie roles, Bara captivated such rulers as Caesar in *Cleopatra* (Gordon Edwards, 1918) and Herod in *Salome* (Gordon Edwards, 1919). In these films, Bara's characters seek to enjoy some of the political power wielded by the male objects of her designing gaze. In the much praised, incipient talkie *Blue Angel* (Josef von Sternberg, 1930), Dietrich's vamp (Lola Lola) seems simply to delight in toying with a respectable professor and reducing him to a shell of a man. She distilled the goal of the role into its essence, pure sexual power for no further purpose such as money, political influence, or revenge.

The femme fatale that interests me is one who maneuvers a bewitched man into killing an unwanted husband. Iconic is Barbara Stanwyck as Phyllis Dietrichson in Billy Wilder's *Double Indemnity* (1944). Not beautiful by conventional standards, Stanwyck's character exudes sex appeal. Flashing her legs, captivating with her eyes, Stanwyck's smoky voice ensnares Fred McMurray as insurance salesman Walter Neff in her dangerous web.[1] The plan is straightforward: Neff will trick the husband into signing a more lucrative insurance policy and then, with Phyllis's help, kill the man. If there is any further deception, it is the uncomplicated, old-fashioned double-cross that Phyllis seems to be planning, thereby eliminating the manipulated accomplice in order to enjoy the full payoff.

The Postman Always Rings Twice (Tay Garnett, 1946) also involves an attractive woman enticing a male stranger into a plot to eliminate her husband in order to reap the insurance money.[2] Only in this case, the boyfriend is unaware of the insurance boondoggle and so is an even bigger sap. Although Stanwyck is the stronger actor, in the later film, Lana Turner (as Cora Smith) offers a variation of the vamp: she is vulnerable and needy more than sexually domineering. A more recent interpretation of the genre finds Nicole Kidman,

DOI: 10.4324/9781003364542-4

34 *The Femme Fatale as Con Artist:* Body Heat

as Suzanne Stone in *To Die For* (Gus Van Sant, 1995), seducing a high school student into murdering her husband. Rather than money, however, Kidman's character just wants the freedom to pursue a career in television.[3]

The femme fatale that I examine here adds a level of imaginative scheming to the linear machinations exhibited by Stanwyck's character. She adds the clever deception of a con game to the murderous plan and thereby makes the protagonist more intelligent, creative, and interesting. More cunning, this femme fatale does not merely hatch a simple theft or insurance scam with the intention of double-crossing her erstwhile lover. It is also a novel twist on the con game genre in which the grifters tend to be men.[4] The femme fatale I consider is not a professional con artist; she does not make her living working marks for money. Consequently, she does not have a troupe of confederates with whom to stage her charade. Rather, her goal is just to make one big killing with one big killing, and to pull it off performing in a solo role. The disarming siren concocts the con so as to make her unsuspecting lover into the fall guy for the death of her spouse. In this way, the "blow off" provides her with an escape hatch out of culpability and into a new life.[5]

Kathleen Turner as Matty plays her con game within the traditional triangular frame of the Stanwyckian femme fatale. She follows the standard plot/ploy: the woman uses her sexual appeal to captivate a male stranger in order to maneuver him into killing her husband for money, an insurance bundle at that. The man is led to believe that he will share in the spoils and live happily ever after with the winsome woman of his erotic dreams. In keeping with more contemporary social mores and cinematic norms, our alluring woman engages in more explicit sexual interaction with her paramour than the femmes fatales of the forties. She is also more blatantly erotic in appearance and banter. But she infuses that standard plotline with a confidence game. As in all con games, Matty uses deception and an entrapping narrative to get money to which she is not entitled. She adds the con game to frame the deceived male accomplice for killing her husband and thereby put herself out of the reach of the long arm of the law, free to enjoy all the ill-gotten gains. And the male chump can only be taken advantage of because of his own moral failings. In this film-story, the femme fatale is smarter and more psychologically astute than virtually all the men (and women) with whom she interacts. As with our other films, the story is constructed so that we, in the audience, discover the con at the same time as the blighted boyfriend. The imminence of the revelation of the grand ploy gives us a jolt akin to what the betrayed paramour experiences.[6]

In *Body Heat* (Lawrence Kasdan, 1981), Matty Walker begins work on her elaborate "long" con well before the action of the film occurs. It involves research, legal knowledge, and assuming a false identity (even with her spouse). When we meet her, Matty is in the process of setting up a lawyer, Ned Racine (William Hurt), known for bungling wills. The con is completed when Matty arranges a deadly trap that she knows Ned will evade, leaving herself as its purported victim. Its denouement requires the façade of Matty

The Femme Fatale as Con Artist: Body Heat   35

underestimating her mark by appearing to commit a fatal mistake. Ned is tricked into believing (erroneously) that he has seen through Matty's hoax. Matty has also led her dupe-lover to think that the murder itself as well as its implementation are his idea. He appears to be the instigator and brains behind the plan.

Our modern-day femme fatale, then, is a formidable woman. As in the standard love triangle, she uses her sensual attraction like a fine instrument to entrap and then control the smitten colluder. She betrays her husband for the sake of great monetary gain, and then traduces her former lover. But where Stanwyck's Phyllis Dietrichson makes do with erotic seduction and an intended double-cross of Walter Neff, Matty informs her sexual conquest with an ingenious con game. Her femme fatale is three steps ahead of her gulled paramour, demonstrating that the "weaker" sex may well be stronger in every way that counts when it comes to larceny and duplicitousness.[7]

Film Noir

The femme fatale is certainly not involved in every noir film and she sometimes casts her spell in films that do not fit the noir bill. Nevertheless, the femme fatale is perhaps most at home in film noir and the web of noir is often most finely spun by her. Consequently, an overview of film noir should be helpful in putting the contemporary femme fatale in a wider cinematic context. This suggestion is reinforced by the fact that film scholars categorize *Body Heat* and *The Last Seduction* (John Dahl, 1994) as "neo-noir:" more recent films that appear to share lineage with classic noir despite diverging in several respects (Conrad 2006: 27). Indeed, the pivotal role of the femme fatale in these films is a major reason for viewing them as neo-noir in the first place.[8]

As the notion of film noir can encompass a vast terrain of movies, there seems to be reasonable disagreement concerning a definition of the concept or whether the films constitute a viable genre. Despite such lack of consensus, Elizabeth Cowie's down to earth observation seems right: "If film noir is not a genre, it is nevertheless recognizable" (1993: 129). Consequently, I shall modestly offer what I think makes it recognizable: a workable characterization that highlights what is both typical and distinctive of the movies that strike most viewers and critics as noir. I readily acknowledge that some of these features are liable to be missing from this or that exemplar of noir and that few of the noir films are likely to have all of these features. We can think of the films designated by noir as sharing a "family resemblance."[9] Let's begin with its origin in French criticism and the written story, and then move on to the characterization.

The French journalist, Nino Frank, coined the term for films because of their resemblance to a class of dark novels, *serie noire* (Pippin, 2012: 5). Subsequent French critics helped establish the term and concept, in particular,

36   *The Femme Fatale as Con Artist:* Body Heat

in reference to American films during the heyday of film noir, its "classic" embodiment in the 1940s and 1950s.[10] These films, such as *The Maltese Falcon* (John Huston, 1941), and *Murder, My Sweet* (Edward Dmytryk, 1944), were often inspired by or based on the detective novels of such writers as Dashiell Hammett and Raymond Chandler. They featured tough-sounding, "hard-boiled" private eyes who investigate a murder, often leaving several strands of the plot at loose ends.

It does seem that virtually all noir films involve crime and the crime is itself cast in a dirty world of gutters, shadows, and rain. "This style is characterized by low-key lighting, chiaroscuro effects of light and shade and unusual shadow patterns... unconventional camera positions... cityscapes of rain-soaked streets at night..." (Brookes, 2017: 35). Critics naturally draw our attention to what might be considered the "atmospherics" of film noir, emphasizing the mood created by dramatic lighting. Through such visual elements as "gleaming silhouettes that loom up in the midst of darkness, shafts of light through Venetian blinds or revolving fans, the flare of a match or a street-lamp piercing through the fog" noir lighting confers "a corporeal presence on space" (Gustafson, 2013: 51). In the grimy urban settings, even interior shots were often shadowy and threatening, noticeably cramped and ominous. The dark settings mirrored the bleak stories: "Hollywood lighting grew darker, character more corrupt, themes more fatalistic and the tone more hopeless" (Schrader, 1996: 53). The overall mood or ambience of these films is one of pessimism; in the words of Robert Porfirio, "despair, loneliness and dread" (1996: 78).

Mark Conrad sees noir as reflecting a world in which objective, permanent values and standards have been eroded. The result is a sense of disorientation and nihilism (2006: 18). The criminals, their victims, and the detectives occupy a world in which good and evil are themselves thrust into the shadows, in which much human choice and action is difficult to praise or condemn. Film noir emphasizes "man's contingency in a world where there are no ... moral absolutes, a world devoid of meaning but the one man himself creates" (Porfirio, 1996: 81). We might say that noir replaces the morally firm ground of earlier, more traditional film-stories with shifting sands.

In such a grim, disillusioned world, the protagonist devolves into an anti-hero. Gone are the clear-cut, unequivocal champions of Westerns, war films, whodunits, or old-fashioned melodramas. Instead, film noir is "populated by anti-heroes whose virtues are often cunning, craftiness, skill in deception and a kind of ruthlessness, and the narratives are saturated with irony" (Pippin, 2012: 10). Jason Holt goes so far as to make the seriously flawed protagonist an essential feature of noir: "Without a hero or heroine of ambiguous moral standing, noir simply evaporates" (2006: 24). Here, we might add that moral ambiguity pervades the film-story and is not just confined to the protagonist.

The anti-hero seems hemmed in by circumstances, to himself as well as to us in the audience. His alienation accompanies a sense of being trapped,

The Femme Fatale as Con Artist: Body Heat   37

a fatalism. The individual fears being overwhelmed by forces beyond his control yet still must make decisions and act (Pippin, 2012: 17). Doing something irrational while still knowing that it is irrational impels people to self-deception; they must excuse or conceal from themselves their weakness. Indeed, weakness in all its manifestations (such as insecurity, avarice, lust, cruelty) seems predominant in film noir; but instead of being resolved in a morally satisfying way, it is left unmitigated, unrepaired. Such hallmarks of stylistic technique as flashback and voice-over reinforce the sense of fatalism. The former creates the impression that the protagonist's present straits were inexorably determined by the past events (depicted in the flashbacks). Because there is no suspense, and "We are watching what has already gone wrong," the retrospective unspooling provides the audience with "the ugly specifics of the way in which these two people ruin their lives and those of others" (Luhr, 2012: 4). The voice-over draws the audience into the narrator's resignation to his looming demise, his foretold plight. William Luhr perceptively describes the impact of informing flashback with voice-over this way: "Their retrospective narrations recount the failures of a past that is already unchangeable. This narrative strategy infuses everything it presents with the aura of inevitable extinction" (29). In short, we share the narrated outlook as the presentation of flawed characters without a future creates a pervasive mood of inevitability and despair.[11]

Locating the basis for the darkness of noir in life rather than in cinematic bent, Holt argues that its perspective is actually more realistic than the more upbeat, hitherto typical Hollywood view of life. He points out that moral ambiguity, flawed protagonists, and disappointing endings are more true to life than tidy, uplifting yarns. "Not only the settings, but also the scenes, the action, the depiction of violent crime, and the characters involved are all quite realistic by and large." (24). Viewing noir as the realistic antidote to the saccharine depictions found in most cinematic fare, Carl Richardson concurs, "The real world *is* shadowy, crime-ridden, web-like, amoral, illogical" (1992: 19). Perhaps downbeat, gloomy endings to episodes or whole narratives are, after all, more like the life most people live. If accurate, then we should include a certain strain of realism in our characterization of noir.

This brings us back to our central figure, the femme fatale herself, and her dynamic place in film noir. First, who or what exactly is this woman? Ian Brookes sees her as "literally, 'deadly woman,' - the predatory, treacherous, and duplicitous figure of the sexual temptress" (2017: 67). She is alluring and, partly for this reason, puts men in jeopardy. E. Ann Kaplan nicely epitomizes the personae of the femmes fatales: in the emerging noir cinema, they are now "defined by their sexuality... desirable but dangerous to men" (1998: 2–3). Perhaps most enticing, she remains a mystery, most saliently for the man who is imperiled by his attraction to her and the crime she lures him into. "She never really is what she seems to be. She harbors a threat which is not entirely legible, predictable, manageable" (Doane, 1991: 1).

38 *The Femme Fatale as Con Artist:* Body Heat

Noir films situate this irresistible, dangerous, mysterious woman at the heart of their plots. As the driver of their films' drama, she is no longer peripheral, ancillary to men as wife, mother, girlfriend, or prostitute. Rather, the femme fatale is "central to the intrigue of the films" (Kaplan 16). Yvonne Tasker cites Phyllis Dietrichson as a paradigm of the desirable, scheming woman who is the decisive actor in *Double Indemnity*, precipitating the plot. Tasker says of Phyllis that "she is the locus of the film's action and a figure of amoral greed" (2008: 355). For all its bleakness, film noir is innovative in elevating women to a position of control – over the tale as well as over its men. The power of these women derives in large part from their brains: "the [noir] films made them the intellectual equals, if not superiors, of the men, perhaps for the first time in film history" (Luhr, 2012: 31). Epitomizing the wily seductress in noir, Janey Place notes that it is "one of the few periods of film in which women are active, not static symbols, are intelligent and powerful, if destructively so, and derive power, not weakness, from their sexuality" (1998: 47). The femmes fatales in our two neo-noir films amplify this representation by exhibiting even greater intelligence than their counterparts in classical noir. Their ability to fashion con games, both elaborate and spontaneous, attests to their intellectual superiority to all the males, indeed, all the other characters, with whom they interact.

Robert Pippin connects the power of the femme fatale to her prey's sense of loss of agency and fatalism. He argues that the captivated male, in fact, appeals to the woman's hold on him to excuse what he knows to be compromised, if not immoral, conduct (51). In this way, the strength of the enticing woman is used by the male to rationalize his weakness and the inevitability of his collapse. He cites Michael O'Hara in *The Lady from Shanghai* (Orson Wells, 1948) as a paradigm. Michael (Orson Welles) explains his folly as the inevitable result of falling under the spell of Elsa Bannister (Rita Hayworth), saying, "When I start to make a fool of myself, there's very little that can stop me" (Pippin, 2012: 55). A variation on "The devil made me do it," since the femme fatale is, after all, a she-devil.

It is only fitting that the femmes fatales in noir displace the virtuous, if somewhat dull, women who usually serve as the auxiliaries to the leading men. Her dark power usurps the hitherto sunny wholesomeness of the girl-next-door: Barbara Stanwyck eclipsing the likes of Doris Day. As the propulsive force of noir, the femme fatale also undermines the standard image of domestic contentment. In noir "the norm of the bourgeois family becomes markedly absent and unattainable" (Gledhill, 1998: 15). Loss of the happily-ever-after finale is accompanied by loss of marital and familial harmony. We will see how exclusion of the supportive spouse and children is inscribed in our neo-noir tales. In fact, the only child who appears (in *Body Heat*) is a pawn in a twisted moment of the ongoing sexual shenanigans of the femme fatale and her mark-lover.

Indeed, Yvonne Tasker makes much of the sexual interests of the femme fatale herself. Where most emphasis has appropriately scrutinized the way in

The Femme Fatale as Con Artist: Body Heat   39

which the temptress draws the man into her murderous orbit, Tasker zeroes in on her own desires. "It is the figure of the 'femme fatale' which has come to stand for noir's innovative representation of female desire" (2013: 357). Not only does noir break new cinematic ground by putting women at the center of the action and by representing their power and intelligence, but it also gives their own sexual interests prominence. This further erodes the place of family in film. Seeking sexual satisfaction outside of marriage, the femmes fatales are "actively involved in the violent assault on the conventional values of family life" (Harvey, 1998: 43). What we have, then, is a portrait of the femme fatale in noir as seductive and devious, powerful and smart, libidinous and independent. All of these attributes are deepened and heightened when she also fabricates her con games in neo-noir. In doing so, she also upends several tropes of the con game saga. First, movie con games are invariably perpetrated by men, even when they deploy women in their theatrics. In addition, the con game itself is devised to supplant the ugliness of violence with the cleverness of cunning, although the ruse often includes a simulation of mayhem. The femme fatale in our films takes the place of the male as the con artist and unhesitatingly resorts to violence, sometimes with gusto. We will also see how her circumstances and fate depart in interesting ways from that of her incarnations in classic noir.

Identity Theft and Legal Trickery

Walking along a Florida boardwalk at night, Ned Racine, a bumbling lawyer, is stunned by the sight of a sexy blonde woman walking toward him in a clinging dress. He thereby reenacts a fatalistic conceit of classic noir: being captured and subsequently undone by the vision of the spider woman. Updating Stanwyck's leggy descent down a staircase toward the upward gaze of Fred MacMurray, Kathleen Turner (as Matty) instantly has her prey in thrall. As Robert Pippin aptly remarks, "femme fatale entrances in noirs often suggest the extreme view of a magical spell or mysterious erotic power that can render the male forever afterward a mere dupe" (2012: 29).[12] Where Walter Neff is mesmerized by Phyllis's anklet, Ned will later exclaim, "That dress!" Ned makes a cute overture to which Matty coyly replies that she is a married woman who is not looking for company. During the ensuing palaver, Matty smiles and tosses her hair provocatively. Having suggested flavored ice from a vendor instead of the drink Ned has proffered, Matty purposely spills some of it on her dress. Ned goes to fetch a paper towel offering to wipe it off and Matty purrs, "You don't want to lick it?" Ned does a perfect double-take, ending in an awe-slapped gawk. When he returns to the boardwalk, Matty has disappeared: beckoning but hard to get.

Some days later, Ned tracks Matty down in a bar in a neighboring, upscale town. After chatting awhile, Matty pretending to discourage her already smitten mark, Ned follows her home in his car, ostensibly to hear the chimes on her porch. Upstairs in her palatial house, Ned touches her face. Matty closes

40 *The Femme Fatale as Con Artist:* Body Heat

her eyes in a mini-swoon, but turns away and tells him to leave. She stands smoldering inside, in view, while Ned paces around the locked home. He finally smashes in a glass door and Matty gasps in a combination of alarm and desire and they embrace fiercely. They make passionate love, a culmination of their building flirtation and banter.

Ensuing scenes of sexual intimacy that punctuate the film find a rhythmic counterpoint in a series of relaxed diner episodes. Ned eats and chats with his friend and sometime legal adversary, Peter Lowenstein (Ted Danson), the assistant district attorney for the county. They are often joined by Oscar (J.A. Preston), a policeman. It is ironic that Ned's two best friends are in law enforcement as he is soon to become a felon. When Ned will not reveal his latest girlfriend, at Matty's insistence, Lowenstein jokes that he has been "living vicariously off" him for years. Lowenstein had previously noted that it has finally dawned on him that Ned uses his professional (legal) incompetence "as a weapon." As the story unfolds, we see that Lowenstein is unflaggingly good-humored but observant and wary on Ned's behalf. We also realize that Matty has herself planned to use Ned's incompetence as a weapon to reap all the riches from her husband's estate and leave Ned holding the bag for her husband's death.

After several earlier trysts with Matty, one evening Ned approaches a blonde woman with her back to him in the gazebo on Matty's property. Thinking it is Matty, Ned jokingly asks, "Hey lady, you want to fuck?" But when she turns around, it is not Matty, although pretty enough to be her sister. She coolly responds, "Gee, I don't know... Maybe." She smiles. Ned is taken aback by his mistake and apologizes. The woman says, "You mean the offer is no good?" Ned admits to feeling like a jerk. Matty saunters over and introduces the woman as Mary Ann. Mary Ann notes, "Ned made me feel very welcome," and indicates that she is leaving after Matty hands her an envelope (later shown to be significant). Matty reassures the unnerved Ned that Mary Ann is an old friend who wants her to be happy.

After more love-making, Matty feigns being afraid to discuss her husband's wealth because when she thinks about it, she wishes "he'd die." As in all cons, Matty is playing a role, inveigling Ned into the scheme that she had cooked up before arranging to meet him. Ned affirms Matty's desire, saying, "That's what we're both thinking. How good it would be for us if he was gone." Matty coyly protests, "No Ned. Please, don't. Don't talk about it." Ned naively dismisses the talk as just that since there is nothing (physically) wrong with Matty's spouse. The conversation takes place in a shadowy, misty undetermined space, as if the revelations need to be shrouded in secrecy. Matty will later disclose that a prenuptial agreement leaves her with practically nothing should she and Edmund (Richard Crenna) divorce. Matty innocently asks Ned to tell her that money would not matter to their future together. Ned chortles and admits he would love her "to be loaded," but assures her that it does

The Femme Fatale as Con Artist: Body Heat   41

not really matter. She smiles and kisses Ned as if that resolves the issue and fetchingly adds, "You make me happy."

When Matty and her husband bump into Ned in a restaurant, Edmund invites Ned to join them after Matty claims to have mentioned him as a local lawyer. Besides noting that Matty would not understand his business dealings, ironic given the sophistication of his wife's con game and (soon-to-be-revealed) legal knowledge, Edmund pontificates about the deficiencies of the man Matty had been with when he met her. He points out that many men want wealth but, "Aren't willing to do what's necessary." Ned concurs that guys like that make him sick. With a rueful chuckle, he demeans himself for lack of gumption by confessing that he is himself a lot like that. Ned thereby adds another irony to Edmund's dismissal of Matty's intelligence.

Matty soon shows up at Ned's office, asking to be held and telling Ned how much she loves him. Ned cautions her about being seen together or talking on the phone, "Because we're going to kill him. We both know that." He adds, "It's the only way we can have everything we want, isn't it?" Matty has deftly manipulated Ned into thinking that he is in charge. To us, it certainly seems as though he has decided to take up Edmund's implicit challenge by no longer being the sickening sort who "cannot do what is necessary." Matty later laments that Edmund's will gives half his considerable wealth to his niece and suggests getting ahold of the document and modifying it. After all, she notes, as a lawyer, Ned would have no trouble making the necessary alterations; however, Ned quashes the idea: "Nothing strange can happen in his life right now. Not one thing out of the ordinary." Although Matty seems to agree that she should not be greedy, secretly changing the will on her own not only leaves her all the money, but is needed to pin the murder on Ned. It is an essential ingredient in Matty's con game, one that neither Ned nor we, in the audience, appreciate yet.

The niece and Edmund's sister represent a semblance of family, but are, of course, financial antagonists to Matty who is bent on thwarting Edmund's generosity toward them. When Edmund's niece stays over at the house, with her uncle out of town, she has a glancing exposure to Matty and Ned in romantic mode. Juxtaposing Edmund's family with Matty's erotic life captures how the femme fatale's power and sexuality oppose even a fragment of familial care and comfort. In an understated manner, then, the film bears out two significant dimensions of classic femmes fatales noted above. First, the way in which the vamp undermines the credibility of domestic bliss; second, and complementing the first, noir's novel depiction of women's independent sexual desire and their ability to realize it.

Next, we see Ned fiddling with an incendiary device as he listens to advice from Teddy Lewis (Mickey Rourke), an arsonist whom Ned once legally represented in a criminal case. Teddy offers to rig the explosive himself, warning Ned that there are myriad ways for any crime to get fouled up. Teddy adds,

42   *The Femme Fatale as Con Artist:* Body Heat

"This arson is serious crime." After killing Edmund in his home, Ned will transport him to "The Breakers," an abandoned resort that Edmund and his partners own. Ned drives down to Miami to conduct some business, stays in a hotel and then rents a car to take him back to Matty's house for the murder. The trip to Miami is supposed to be Ned's cover or alibi for the night of the murder. A slight hitch in timing requires Ned to scuffle with Edmund before finally killing him, unloading him in The Breakers, and setting the place on fire.

The film uses heat as a running motif. Besides this bit of arson and another toward the end of the film, at the story's beginning Ned watches a distant fire from his window. Throughout the film story, temperatures in Florida are high, and Matty's body itself runs hotter than normal. Then too, the torrid sexual couplings themselves are hot stuff, literally and figuratively. The suggestion is that the steamy charms of the femme fatale overwhelm the dupe, addling his brain so as to keep him from realizing what is happening to him. Only in the cool remove of a prison cell will Ned finally come to his senses and piece together the elements of Matty's complex scam. Before then she will implicate him in Edmund's death by tinkering with her husband's will, unbeknownst to the unsuspecting Ned.

Edmund's lawyer soon arranges for a meeting to discuss Edmund's altered will, purportedly modified by Ned himself. Besides Ned, Matty and Edmund's sister, Lowenstein is there pursuing an investigation into Edmund's death. The reworking of the will, however, has been sloppy, rendering it invalid according to Florida law. The upshot is that Matty, pretending to be confused and surprised, inherits everything, leaving Edmund's niece out in the cold. The result is just as good as if the will had formally excluded the niece, but more plausible given Edmund's known wish to provide for his niece.[13] Matty has perceptively played upon Ned's history of incompetence, alluded to acerbically by Edmund's lawyer. We, in the audience, had been alerted to Ned's slipshod legal work by an early scene in which a judge chides him for barely mounting a defense of his shady client's half-baked attempt at fraud. Recall that we also heard Lowenstein gently joking that he finally realized that Ned was using his "incompetence as a weapon." Along with Ned, we will subsequently learn that Matty had been told about Ned's bungling of a similar will creation in the Gourson case. Matty has boxed Ned in because he cannot deny that he rewrote Edmund's will, given that Matty has forged his signature.

"Matty's" Triumph

Waiting in his home are Ned's law enforcement buddies. Lowenstein and Oscar are leery of Matty and inform Ned that Edmund's group, who owned The Breakers, are a "rough crowd" – referring to their reputation for violently seasoned crime. When Lowenstein warns Ned off Matty, calling her "very bad news," Ned insists that he is interested in her. His friends see and tell Ned the truth about Matty, a truth he cannot or will not let himself see, because they are not enthralled by her. Matty will shortly confess to Ned to altering the will purposely, having worked in a law office, but (falsely) deny knowing about Ned's stumbling track record. She will also, insincerely, echo his friends' alarmed chorus, asserting that if Ned never trusted her again, he would "probably be smart." She beguilingly adds, "I love you. And I need you."

Ned soon learns that the police have not found Edmund's glasses in the remains of the fire, indicating that he was likely killed elsewhere and taken to the resort – which, of course, is exactly what happened. This weakens the narrative that Matty and Ned have been shaping, namely, that Edmund somehow got caught up in foul play at the derelict resort itself. However, their false account could be plausible because Lowenstein and Oscar have told Ned (and the audience) that Edmund is mixed up with dangerous people. He is himself morally unsavory, "willing to do what's necessary." Edmund's moral turpitude adds to the moral ambiguity that is a hallmark of classical *noir*. Of course, Matty and Ned are murderers; however, they are ridding the world of a gangster! Matty suggests to Ned that the maid may have the glasses and probably is holding out for hush money. The final stage of Matty's con game will, in fact, be a playing out of this additional fabrication.

Lowenstein can be viewed as a subtly placed foil for Ned. Wary and careful, where Ned is impulsive and sloppy, Lowenstein exhibits a lighthearted grace that suggests a self-awareness that Ned also lacks. Awaiting Ned on a deserted evening pier, Lowenstein cavorts alone under a streetlight, entertaining himself with a flowing, whimsical dance. The dance echoes Lowenstein's sashaying out of the trio's regular diner earlier in the film and resonates with his two humorous comments about Ned. The comments tie together Ned's salient tendencies of sexual adventure and legal fumbling, both of which Matty ingeniously exploits. Lowenstein does not take himself, or his terpsichore, very seriously, but he knows who he is (dancing while realistically grounded) in a way that Ned does not. When Ned shows up (paradoxically smoking after a healthful run), Lowenstein informs him that an unknown person is trying to give them Edmund's missing glasses and that someone called Ned's hotel room in Miami the night Edmund was killed, but the phone rang on unanswered. Plainly, somebody is trying to tie Ned to Edmund's death. Lowenstein obviously suspects Ned of criminal involvement and is trying to warn him of his growing legal danger.

Ned's suspicions about Matty are further aroused by a conversation he happens to have with the opposing the lawyer from the Gourson case. The attorney informs Ned that he had given Ned's name to an attractive woman he had met at a party and may, in fact, have mentioned the disastrous case to her. So far, however, this looks like the standard double-cross, albeit with added strata of deceit.

44   *The Femme Fatale as Con Artist:* Body Heat

Further compounding Ned's growing concern about his lover is information conveyed by Teddy Lewis, Ned's arson-loving, former client. He tells Ned that a woman meeting Matty's description visited him, using Ned as a reference. The attractive woman had told him that Ned wanted another fire, "She had me show her how to rig it [the incendiary contraption] to a door, with a little delay." Teddy adds that the police have been questioning him about The Breakers, as he is a known flame purveyor. As if confirming Ned's growing suspicions, Matty calls him, ostensibly from Miami, to tell him that she had to pay off the maid. She adds that the glasses are to be put by the maid in the boathouse adjoining her home and encourages Ned to retrieve them soon as she does not trust the maid. Although Ned has his doubts, due to the accumulation of information that incriminates Matty as sabotaging him, her story sounds plausible enough to get him to go to the boathouse.

We come now to the explosive climax of the plot, but not its denouement. In the dark, Ned checks out the boathouse: peering in the windows, circling the building nervously. At last, he does discover an ominous-looking wire. Matty shows up, a good deal later than she had promised and says, "It's all ours now. We could leave tonight if we wanted to." She is surprised to see Ned holding the gun of Edmund's he has retrieved from her house and asks, "What's happened?" Ned tells her that he did not see the glasses and Matty is forced to admit that she arranged to meet him because of his history of shoddy will work, but that everything changed when she fell in love with him. When Ned challenges her to fetch the glasses, Matty heads off to the boathouse, saying that no matter what happens, "I do love you." Along with Oscar who has shown up to arrest him, Ned watches the boathouse burst into flames.[14]

Lying in his bunk in jail, Ned's eyes pop open and he exclaims, "She's alive." He proceeds to relate to Oscar his (accurately pieced together) account of Matty's con game. Oscar points out that the dental records prove that the woman's body in the boathouse is that of Matty Tyler. Ned suggests that the woman could be her friend and that it is the friend after all who is the real "Matty Tyler." The woman he has known as "Matty" may, in fact, be the real Mary Ann and she has had to pay off the friend for assuming her name as an alias. Recall that we saw Ned's Matty give an envelope to her alleged friend Mary Ann at the gazebo adjacent to her home. We now realize why the scene is so important. Even as Ned mistook the woman who was apparently Mary Ann for Matty, so will he, and everyone else, take the real Mary Ann to be the woman named "Matty." The switched identity (or identity theft) is now disclosed as vital to the con into which Mary Ann (aka "Matty') smoothly slides Ned. The false identity emblematizes an essential element in all flimflam: the con artist is never who or what the mark thinks she is. She is always playing a role: here, Mary Ann Simpson playing the role of "Matty Tyler."

Just as neo-noir modifies some of the ingredients found in its classical form, so does it also play with the classic con game film. As indicated above, a woman is now the con artist, not a man. In addition, as the woman

The Femme Fatale as Con Artist: Body Heat   45

is a femme fatale, she embraces violence. The standard con game eschews violence, replacing its coarseness with the inventiveness of the deceptive scheme. Matty even goes so far to arrange for the death of her alleged friend, the real "Matty" whose body is discovered in the burnt-out boathouse. We are left to wonder how exactly Mary Ann (aka "Matty") got her erstwhile friend into the boathouse and whether she had had to kill her to do so. In the event, the murderous Matty has been ruthless. Besides arranging for her husband's demise, she is responsible for killing someone whom she warmly described as a long-time friend and who has, undoubtedly, facilitated her con game by "lending" Mary Ann her identity. In our other neo-noir film, *The Last Seduction* (John Dahl, 1994), Bridget also has recourse to violence in augmenting her con, only in her case she will energetically do the deed herself.

The accurate scenario that Ned offers smacks of the time-honored device of the smart detective explaining to characters in the film-story how the villain executed his crime, thereby revealing the mystery's intricacies to the audience. We may well wonder whether Ned is bright enough to have unraveled Matty's deadly grift. No matter. With the planned explosion, "Matty" eliminates the real Matty Tyler and frames Ned for the murder. She also puts herself in the clear, the classic "blow off" of the con game. After all, Ned could not have murdered Edmund by himself, but Matty is now neatly out of the picture – having apparently perished in the boathouse flames. Although there could be some question as to who is supposed to have rigged the arson device in the boathouse, it is feasible to see it construed as Ned's (putatively successful) attempt to get rid of the woman known to all as "Matty." He would have done this in order to keep all of Edmund's money for himself, thereby mirroring what Matty has actually pulled off. Ned sardonically quotes Edmund, telling Oscar that "Matty" was the kind of person who "could do what was necessary."

Ned's conjecture is soon confirmed by a copy of the school's yearbook in which we see that the real Matty Tyler looks like a younger version of the woman earlier identified as Mary Ann at the gazebo and that Ned's "Matty" is, in fact, Mary Ann Simpson. Her black and white photo gives way to the present day "Matty" reclining on a sunny beach with a new beau. Matty has gradually led Ned to kill her husband, in the classic manner of the femme fatale film noir movie. However, she has maneuvered her boyfriend by means of a carefully crafted con game. She uses Ned's error-ridden track record as a lawyer along with her own legal expertise to frame him for the murder. The stray ends of the scheme are then neatly tied up by her fake identity in concert with the demise of the real Matty Tyler. In the *noir* tradition of Stanwyck's Phyllis, Matty lures her lover into doing away with her husband; however, where Phyllis ultimately fails (and dies), Matty makes off with the insurance bundle and escapes into a new, and tropically sunny, life. The suggestion here is that the con game has provided Matty with the needed supplement to the

46 *The Femme Fatale as Con Artist:* Body Heat

standard vamp's devices. She is successful precisely because she has framed her seductive manipulation with a brilliant bit of flimflam.

Notes

1 For a male counterpart, think of John Malkovich. Not handsome by any stretch of the imagination, he is nevertheless, convincing as a witty, seductive serial paramour in *Dangerous Liaisons* (Stephen Frears, 1988).

2 Leslie Margolin argues persuasively in *Murderess!* that the two novels written by John M. Cain on which the film-stories of *Double Indemnity* and *The Postman Always Rings Twice* are based, were themselves patterned after the real-life killing performed by Ruth Snyder and Judd Gray in 1927 (New York: Kensington Publishing Corp., 1999).

3 At the risk of omitting one or more of the readers' favorites, here are a few more gems of cinematic femmes fatales and the noir films in which they exercised their sensual power: Kathie Moffat (Jane Greer) in Jacques Tourneur's *Out of the Past* (1947); Rita Hayworth as the title character in *Gilda* (Charles Vidor, 1946) and as Elsa Bannister in Orson Welles's *The Lady from Shanghai (*1948); Joan Bennett, as Kitty March in Fritz Lang's *Scarlet Street* (1945). For good measure, we might also consider the eponymous character of *Lolita* (Stanley Kubrick, 1962) played by Sue Lyon, a nymphet (or *jeune fille*) fatale.

4 See, for example, *Nine Queens* (Fabian Belinsky, 2000), *House of Games* (David Mamet, 1987), *The Sting* (George Roy Hill, 1973), and *Matchstick Men* (Ridley Scott, 2003).

5 The blow off is the finishing touch of the con that wraps it up, ideally so neatly that the marks who have been fleeced are unaware that they have been conned at all, as in *The Sting.*

6 In respect to the con game being revealed to the audience at the same time as the duped male realizes what has happened to him, our films are like *Matchstick Men* but unlike *The Sting.* The delight in the latter film includes being in on the con with the grifters.

7 A film that inverts the contours of the femme fatale film is *Dial M for Murder* (Alfred Hitchcock, 1954). Here, the husband seeks to rid himself of his unfaithful wife, but does so with the help of another man on whom he exerts the pressure of blackmail rather than the seductive charm of the femme fatale.

8 Here is a sample of the many more recent films that sport noir credentials: *Chinatown* (John Huston, 1974), *Reservoir Dogs* (Quentin Tarantino, 1992), *Blue Velvet* (David Lynch, 1986), *A Simple Plan* (Sam Raimi, 1998), *Memento* (Christopher Nolan, 2000), and from the Coen Brothers, Joel and Ethan: *Blood Simple* (1984) and *No Country for Old Men* (2007).

9 The term was established by the philosopher Ludwig Wittgenstein (Sections 66–71) and suggests that members of a class of objects, such as games or languages, are related by a series of overlapping similarities rather than an essential set of features that are common to all the members of the class.

10 William Luhr provides a helpful discussion of the work of Raymond Borde and Etienne Chaumerton that was published in 1955 (53–54).

11 Billy Wilder presents an extreme form of this stylistic framing in his 1950 noir *Sunset Boulevard.* Here, the narrator, Joe Gillis (William Holden), is already deceased as he recounts his misadventure, shown floating face-down in a swimming pool.

12 Two notable examples of femmes fatales exerting their seductive influence at first sight in classic noir are Elsa Bannister's (Rita Hayworth) grip on Michael O'Hara (Orson Welles) in *The Lady from Shanghai* (Orson Welles, 1948) and Kathie Moffat

The Femme Fatale as Con Artist: Body Heat 47

(Jane Greer) enthralling Jeff Bailey (Robert Mitchum), shown in flashback, in Jacques Tourneur's *Out of the Past,* 1947.

13 Before the big meeting, Ned goes out of his way to talk with the niece to demonstrate that he is not the man the girl had seen at night with Matty. It provides a moment of additional suspense and Ned's daring is to his chicanerous credit.

14 We had previously seen abbreviated scenes of Oscar investigating Ned's business dealings, hotel stay, and car rental in Miami.

Bibliography

Brookes, Ian (2017). *Film Noir: A Critical Introduction.* London: Bloomsbury.

Conrad, Mark (2006). "Nietzsche and the Meaning and Definition of Noir." In *The Philosophy of Film Noir.* Ed. Mark Conrad. Lexington, KY: University of Kentucky, 7–22.

Cowie, Elizabeth (1993). "Film Noir and Women." In *Shades of Noir.* Ed. Joan Opjec. London: Verso, 121 –166.

Doane, Mary Ann (1991). *Femme Fatales: Feminism, Film Theory, Psychoanalysis.* New York: Routledge.

Gustafson, Henrik (2013). "A Wet Emptiness: The Phenomenology of Film Noir. In *A Companion to Film Noir.* Ed. Andrea Spicer and Helen Hanson. Oxford: Blackwell, 50–66.

Gledhill, Christine (1998). "Klute: A Contemporary Film Noir and Feminist Criticism" (1st of 2 essays). In *Women in Film Noir.* Ed. E. Ann Kaplan. London: BFI, 6–21.

Harvey, Sylvia (1998). "Woman's Place: The Absent Family of Film Noir." In *Women in Film Noir.* Ed. Kaplan, 35–46.

Holt, Jason (2006). "A Darker Shade: Realism in Neo-Noir." In *The Philosophy of Film Noir.* Ed. Mark Conrad, 23–40.

Kaplan, Ann (1998). "Introduction." In *Women in Film Noir.* Ed. Kaplan, 1–14.

Luhr, William (2012). *Film Noir.* Oxford: Wiley-Blackwell.

Pippin, Robert (2012). *Fatalism in American Film Noir: Some Cinematic Philosophy.* Charlottesville: University of Virginia.

Place, Janey (1998). "Women in Film Noir." In *Women in Film Noir.* Ed. Kaplan. 47–68.

Porfirio, Robert (1996). "No Way Out: Existential Motifs in the Film Noir." In *Film Noir Reader.* Ed. Alain Silver and John Ursini. Pompton Plains, NJ: Limelight, 77–93.

Richardson, Carl (1992). *Autopsy: An Element of Realism in Film Noir.* Metuchen, NJ: Scarecrow.

Schrader, Paul (1996). "Notes on Film Noir." In *Film Noir Reader.* Ed. Silver and Ursini, 53–64.

Tasker, Yvonne (2013). "Women in Film Noir." In *A Companion to Film Noir.* Ed. Andrea Spicer and Helen Hanson, 353–368.

Wittgenstein, Ludwig (1956). *Philosophical Investigations.* New York: Macmillan Publishing.

Filmography

Belinsky, Fabian (2000). *Nine Queens.* U.S.

Coen, Ethan and Joel (1984). *Blood Simple.* U.S. (2007).

——— (2007). *No Country for Old Men.* U.S.

48   *The Femme Fatale as Con Artist:* Body Heat

Dahl, John (1994). *The Last Seduction.* UK.

Dmytryk, Edward (1944). *Murder, My Sweet.* U. S.

Edwards, Gordon (1918). *Cleopatra.* U.S.

—— (1919). *Salome.* U.S.

Frears, Stephen (1988). *Dangerous Liaisons.* U.S.

Garnett, Tay (1946). *The Postman Always Rings Twice.* U.S.

Hill, George Roy (1973). *The Sting.* U.S.

Hitchcock, Alfred (1954). *Dial M for Murder.* U.S.

Huston, John (1941). *The Maltese Falcon.* U.S.

—— (1974). *Chinatown.* U.S.

Kasdan, Lawrence (1981). *Body Heat.* U.S.

Kubrick, Stanley (1962). *Lolita.* U.S.

Lang, Fritz (1945). *Scarlet Street.* U.S.

Lynch, David (1986). *Blue Velvet.* U.S.

Mamet, David (1987). *House of Games.* U.S.

Nolan, Christopher (2000). *Memento.* U.S.

Raimi, Sam (1998). *A Simple Plan.* U.S.

Scott, Ridley (2003). *Matchstick Men.* U.S.

Tarantino, Quentin (1992). *Reservoir Dogs.* U.S.

Tourneur, Jacques (1947). *Out of the Past.* U.S.

Van Sant, Gus (1995). *To Die For.* U.S.

Vidor, Charles (1946). *Gilda.* U.S.

von Sternberg, Josef (1930). *Blue Angel.* U.S.

Welles, Orson (1948). *The Lady from Shanghai.* U.S.

Wilder, Billy (1944). *Double Indemnity.* U.S.

—— (1950). *Sunset Boulevard.* U.S.

4 Improvising on the Run

The Last Seduction

A Formidable Woman

In many respects, this chapter continues the discussion begun in the previous chapter. *The Last Seduction* (John Dahl, 1994) features another femme fatale who performs the classic noir magic of manipulating her boyfriend/dupe into (almost) killing her husband in order to abscond with a bundle. As with Matty, Bridget Gregory also fabricates a con game, or two, in the service of achieving her financial goal of stealing from her spouse. As such, the film furthers the exploration of the novel and intriguing synthesis of two cinematic genres: neo-noir and con artist. As with the classic femmes fatales of yesteryear, the spider women of neo-noir must still contend with lack of full access to institutional, economic, and social power. Augmenting the sexual power of their namesakes with con games enables them to compete more fully with and more fully vanquish their male counterparts, cohorts, and antagonists.

As we saw, Matty works out an elaborate long-con into which she adroitly inserts her erotic seduction. She has the time and patience to digest the details of Florida conjugal law, the ineptitude of the lawyer she will entrap, and plan how to stage the fiery finale that will ensure her mark's culpability and her safe escape. Bridget, however, must manufacture a major con game while on the run from her husband, one that will eventuate in his demise. In doing so, she improvises yet another, subordinate ploy to propel her recently acquired paramour into going along with the overarching scheme.

Both women thereby demonstrate dimensions of what, following Aristotle, we can describe as intellectual virtues. Unlike the math and science emphasized by Aristotle, however, the intellectual virtues of our femmes fatales are practical; they include action designed to achieve specific ends, to wit, a great deal of money. So, the intellectual strengths of Matty and Bridget are akin to business acumen. Differences between the two are instructive. Matty possesses a methodical, deliberate intelligence. In the business world, it would enable her to map out a long-term strategy, develop an organizational structure, and implement it over an extended period of production and innovation. Matty has the capacity to assimilate complicated and subtle relationships

DOI: 10.4324/9781003364542-5

50 *Improvising on the Run:* The Last Seduction

among interlocking parts, such as found in law, finance, or government. This is the sort of ability that also enables success in the military and industry. In another time or social world, Matty could well have been a business tycoon, an army general, or the head of a legal firm. But in a world in which women lack the legitimate opportunities afforded men, she resorts to an intricate con game, one that includes the femme fatale's sensual entrapment of an unsuspecting male accomplice.

In Bridget's case, her intellectual virtue includes core staples of practical wisdom, or *phronesis.* The ground of *phronesis* is cleverness, knowing the means to particular ends. This will invariably require understanding human nature: what people prize and how their interests relate to our own pursuits. As Aristotle points out, the degree to which people possess this species of perceptiveness is, to some extent, a matter of the natural endowments of good sense and intelligence (rather than formal education) (1962: 166). A person with practical wisdom is keenly aware of what is transpiring around her and is able to assess the significance of it for her own benefit. As Stanley Godlovitch notes, the individual with *phronesis* has "the ability to draw certain types of conclusion from experience" (1993: 271). Bridget is able to seize upon opportunities as they present themselves rather than examining a host of options and crafting a master plan in a more deliberate manner (as Matty does in *Body Heat*). She foresees the ramifications of appealing courses of action as they arise, and can act decisively, without undue cogitation or trepidation. Chief among Bridget's strengths is the ability to perceive people's weaknesses and act upon them to her advantage. Although we can imagine her doing as well with an individual's strengths, the film centers on the vulnerabilities that Bridget so craftily manages to glean and exploit: whether it be the man she will manipulate into helping her, an insurance manager, or the private eye that her husband hires to root her out.

For Aristotle, Bridget's practical sagacity necessarily falls short of genuine or full practical wisdom because she does not strive for what is virtuous and truly good (Aristotle, 1962: 152). She obviously does not enjoy the further insight and moral character needed to truly comprehend which purposes are good or noble as well as how much different ends are actually worth (Foot, 1993: 219). Bridget only aims for wealth and is willing to do violence to obtain it. Although Bridget lacks the essential, overriding element of appreciating and striving for a virtuous life, we can see how her acumen is vital to practical wisdom. It is most prominently displayed in Bridget's ability to improvise a course of action on the spur of the moment, as new opportunities emerge or as plans go awry.

To improvise is to create a hitherto unscripted sequence of conduct, often in response to an unanticipated event or unforeseen change in circumstance. Familiar examples of improvised behavior include playing a novel musical variation, making a home repair with what is ready to hand or connecting with a sports teammate in an unrehearsed play. The person who improvises

Improvising on the Run: The Last Seduction   51

successfully has recourse to a rich and supple imagination; the language of sight is apt as she foresees, envisions, and pictures. The ability to reconfigure a situation in a fresh way in order to achieve a desirable end is a gift few of us possess. Improvisation does not necessarily require immediate action, but Bridget's innovative scenarios do involve this often-critical element. And the urgency of immediacy makes her improvisations the more remarkable, implemented as they are as spontaneously as they spring to mind, without further ado. It is as if the agility of her mind translates directly into the appropriate course of conduct and, for better or worse, Bridget's action is never delayed (as say Hamlet's is most famously) by compunction, doubt, or complication.

Bridget's powers of improvisation are displayed on at least four occasions: in her two con games and two murders. Bridget cooks up her major con game as soon as she acquires some insurance-based knowledge from her boyfriend/ chump. She immediately grasps the potential to create a phony narrative about killing insured, but philandering, men in order to split their policy's benefits with aggrieved and spiteful female spouses. As is her wont, Bridget then puts her plan straight into action. But when her boyfriend unfortunately has qualms about killing people, Bridget discharges a minor bit of flimflam in order to pressure him into going along with the big scheme (his later squeamishness will force Bridget to improvise the killing of her husband). And this subordinate con itself involves several moments of improvisation, including filching a few props and impersonating a health official, that will be pivotal for Bridget to gain information necessary to fooling her lover. As if this were not enough to burnish Bridget's credentials as a master (or mistress) of improvisation, both the murders that she orchestrates are unplanned and accomplished in the heat of the moment.

To appreciate Bridget's talent for improvisation, compare her ability to imagine a scenario and implement it directly with a cinematic example that seems to more fully embody practical wisdom by serving a noble or virtuous end. I am thinking here of Colonel Joshua Chamberlain's offensive tactic conceived and acted upon amid the hurly-burly of the battle of Little Round Top in the film *Gettysburg* (Ron Maxwell, 1993). The Union forces are depleted, running out of ammunition, and about to be overrun by the surging Rebels. As Chamberlain's troops are the flank of the army on the mountain, if his position is lost, the rest of the Union men will be exposed to the Confederate onslaught. With no time to spare, Chamberlain orders his besieged soldiers to sweep down and over the hill, like "a door." Instead of digging in for a futile last stand, the Colonel has decided to attack! And his tactic is successful, taking the opposition completely by surprise. Like Chamberlain, Bridget has a feel for spontaneous stratagems, puts them directly into action, and takes her opponents by surprise. Unlike the valiant Union Colonel, her ends are totally venal and this would, certainly for Aristotle, disqualify her cognitive strengths as actual *phronesis*.

52 *Improvising on the Run:* The Last Seduction

For her first murder, Bridget finds herself seemingly at the mercy of the private eye whom her husband, Clay, has hired to ferret her out and retrieve the money she has stolen from him. She is driving the car and he is the passenger telling her what to do at gunpoint. Bridget badgers him into taking out his member, citing the reputation of Black men for impressive sexual credentials. Thus exposed, he is killed when Bridget crashes the vehicle, saving herself by dint of the driver's safety airbag. She has initiated this little operation on the spot in response to the unforeseen assault on her wealth. Bridget cites the man's exposed phallus when later talking to a policeman in the hospital where she is recovering from the crash. When her lover is later unable to carry through with his responsibility to kill her husband, Bridget again improvises, however crudely, to realize her ends. In both instances, her nimble imagination expresses itself, without impediment or psychological resistance, in spontaneous, effective action.

With the two murders that Bridget undertakes, we return to the moral vice of ruthlessness, discussed in connection with Matty. Unlike Matty, Bridget is forced by circumstances to dirty her own hands in the killing of her husband and, along the way, in the "accidental" death of her husband's private investigator. This adds a layer to the ruthlessness or cruelty that characterizes Matty. In the previous chapter, we saw that Matty not only inveigles Ned into killing her husband but also arranges for her friend, the real Matty Tyler, to be killed in the film's fiery finale. Maneuvering someone into killing one's spouse is ruthless, but sending the friend whose identity you have borrowed to her death certainly compounds Matty's lack of care or empathy. Nevertheless, she manages to have her wicked deeds done at a distance. It seems to take another level of toughness or bloodthirstiness to actually perform the fatal act, something like the difference between poisoning someone who dies hours later and strangling the person with one's bare hands. We might consider this a species of lack of inhibition for violating humanity in a grisly manner. This capacity for direct, unmediated violence, then, amplifies Bridget's vice of ruthlessness. It makes her seem even more monstrous than Matty. Yet even here, the film manages to be artful. Bridget's full participation in horrific killing is dramatically juxtaposed with her agile hatching of con games: the brute physicality of the former contrasting with the subtle cognitive dexterity of the latter.

The subjugation of women frames the sexual power displayed by femmes fatales in both classic noir and neo-noir. Women who are trapped in loveless marriages to stodgy, apparently older men do not see how they can make their way without a spouse or divorce, and the latter is itself an unsavory option for social as well as financial reasons. Getting what they want depends on men: first their husbands, then their lovers. Although the more modern iteration of the deadly woman does seem to have more options than her predecessors, she is still depicted as subordinate to men, deprived of the full array of social and economic avenues available to males. She is lacking in institutionalized sanctioned power. The films I am examining underline the inferior status of

Improvising on the Run: The Last Seduction   53

their femmes fatales through male denigration: explicit and symbolic. Recall Edmund's disparaging of Matty's ability to understand the machinations of his (legally questionable) business ventures only for him to be undone by her, including flouting his posthumous financial wishes for his sister and niece. Then, too, all the men in the film underestimate Matty's cunning. The abasement of women in *The Last Seduction* is more symbolic, but more blatant as well.

Bridget is struck in the face at the outset and conclusion of the film, first by her husband Clay and then by her boyfriend Mike. Although the first bit of violence may not be the impetus for Bridget's theft of the marital money, it nevertheless symbolizes Clay's status. When Mike hits her at the film's murderous climax, it is the prelude to sexually assaulting her, a further signifier of male control. Clay also belittles Bridget's murderous attempt by mocking her accomplice as lacking the gumption to carry out his lethal role. Accompanying these physical demonstrations of male force are the references to phallic size, an almost cliched insignia of male valorization. Mike advertises his endowment as a come-on to Bridget when they first meet in a bar, and Bridget uses the popular belief about Black men to persuade the private eye to expose himself. But male sexual organs are directly related to physical penetration of women: the bigger they are the more in control, at least as men may view the relationship. In this regard, the movie can be interpreted as being ironic. For all of Mike's grandeur below the belt, Bridget leads him by the nose thoroughly and throughout their relationship. Moreover, his masculine pride is itself virtually undermined by mistakenly marrying a male transvestite. What a comeuppance, or comedown, for someone whose virility can be so boastfully measured!

Bridget's genius lies in fashioning her flimflam on the spur of the moment, in the midst of betraying and fleeing her husband. Only after she seduces Mike and is subsequently hunted down by a private eye hired by her husband does Bridget devise a con to eliminate her spouse and put the blame on her new lover. She uses insurance information supplied by her boyfriend to create a murder narrative plausible enough for Mike to find credible but repugnant. To push him into the role of killer, Bridget uses knowledge harvested from her mini-con. Even when the actual murderous deed goes awry, Bridget manages to improvise the execution as well as make Mike the fall guy and thereby extricate herself from the situation, scot free and wealthy.

Con Artist on the Lam

The Last Seduction begins with a simple intra-marital theft: Bridget Gregory (Linda Fiorentino) absconds with the $700,000 that her husband, Clay (Bill Pullman), has received from peddling pharmaceutical cocaine on the black market. A resident physician in a hospital, Clay has had to borrow $100,000 from gangsters to finance the illegal transaction and is now, at home, pulling

54   *Improvising on the Run:* The Last Seduction

out packets of bills stuffed in his shirt because the drug buyers have left him without a briefcase. When Bridget calls him an idiot for walking the streets in such clumsy fashion, Clay gives her a crisp, backhand slap to the face. He immediately apologizes, explaining his untoward behavior as a case of nerves in the aftermath of his perilous transaction. That this nasty outburst is Bridget's motivation for taking off with the haul while Clay showers is questionable as she has a car at the ready under an NYC bridge, duplicating the location of Clay's recent sale. The bridges may symbolize how the arc of the story begins and ends with Bridget's exit and return to the Big Apple.

Nevertheless, we should not discount the dramatic significance of the slap. Even though Bridget is clearly a forceful, capable woman, she is still at a disadvantage in the social, financial world; it is dominated by men. As with her femmes fatales forbears, Bridget will have recourse to sexual attraction to get what she wants by manipulating men. The physical display of power or pique, then, is placed as symbolic of male control, even if, in this instance, it is not, in fact, the motivation for Bridget's marital betrayal.

Stopping in the small Pennsylvania town of Beston, Bridget goes into a bar where Mike (Peter Berg) is telling two friends that he is not happy to be back home but things just did not work out in Buffalo, New York (about an hour's drive north from Beston). One of the friends impishly alludes to Mike getting married in Buffalo, a fact that will prove pivotal to the smaller con game that Bridget will play on Mike. Mike reprises the instant intoxication that foretold Ned's perilous relationship with Matty, when he soon has his "Wow Moment" at the sight of Bridget. In fact, Mike actually says "Wow!" when, in a short, tight-fitting skirt, Bridget demands of the churlish, unresponsive bartender, "Who does a girl have to suck around here to get a drink!" Ian Brookes reminds us of the femme fatale's irresistible sorcery as a staple of noir: "The initial appearance of a femme fatale in a noir narrative is invariably beguiling" (2017: 71). Mike helps Bridget get her drink and after being rebuffed by her tries to impress her with the size of his manhood. Bridget astonishes him by immediately checking out his equipment under the booth's table, quizzing him on his sexual history, and arranging to go to his place for sex. We know from an early scene as foreman at a phone sales center that Bridget is a tough, take-charge woman. Her work in phone sales is the perfect model of her dealing with Mike: size up the customer, make a quick, clipped pitch, and close the deal. Unlike many femmes fatales, including Matty, Bridget will dominate in the relationship with no pretense of neediness or fostering the illusion that the boyfriend is taking the lead. She will, of course, use her erotic appeal to pull Mike into her plan and hold out the possibility of a loving, shared future.

Recall Yvonne Tasker's observation that the femme fatale opens up new movie possibilities by underscoring the woman's own erotic desires (2013). Not only does she play upon her male sidekick's lust for her, but she uses him to fulfill her own libidinous needs. In our neo-noir film stories, the woman's sexuality is made more explicit and pervasive than could be countenanced in

Improvising on the Run: The Last Seduction 55

the decades (especially 1940s) of the classical movies. Throughout *The Last Seduction,* Bridget will unabashedly demand sexual satisfaction and threaten to abandon Mike for a future sex partner should he become too unruly or demanding. Matty also seems to enjoy her multiple liaisons with Ned and it is telling that at the film's conclusion, we get a partial view of her new plaything hovering by her chaise lounge as she basks in a tropical clime. As with Bridget, Matty's lust adds sexual autonomy to her impressive intellect and willpower.

After the first of several scenes of torrid love-making, Bridget calls a trusted lawyer in New York. He advises her to stay put and keep the bundle she has taken from Clay in cash until after the divorce, as her husband would be entitled to half of hard assets, such as real estate. Bridget soon secures a job in an insurance company that is commensurate with her experience, telling her new boss that she has to use a fake name because she has had to leave her abusive husband (a narrative she will employ again in conning Mike). As with Mike and virtually all other men in the film, Bridget is always found to be credible. Playing a role, or several, is necessary to being a successful con artist and although Bridget has not yet begun conning Mike, her thespian skills are on display. She tells the insurance administrator who is interviewing her that she will go by the name "Wendy Kroy." Excising the "dy" in Wendy leaves "New York" backward, a variant that Clay will later deduce due to his knowledge of Bridget's knack for writing backward. And indeed, she signs her work contract with it upside down, facing the gullible executive who has just hired her.

Discovering that Mike works at the same insurance company, Bridget tells him that if she had known she was going to remain in the town she would not have had anything to do with him. Bridget wants him to forget about their one-night stand, saying, "I work here now. Don't fuck with my image." The lawyer soon tells her to send Clay some money who is in danger by virtue of owing the loan sharks $10,000 in interest on his initial loan. She calls her husband person-to-person but hangs up when he asks the operator if the call is from Chicago or Dallas. When she later calls, Clay will have a Black private investigator, Harlan, available to trace the call. They are able to track only the area code before a suspicious Bridget terminates that call, but, figuring out her alias, Clay confidently sends Harlan on the road to find her.

Bridget soon has abandoned sex with Mike against a fence, behind their regular bar. Mike asks her where he fits into her life and Bridget/Wendy crudely dismisses him as her "designated fuck." When Mike asks what if he wants more than that, Bridget replies, "Then I'll designate someone else." This is just one of many telling scenes during which Bridget most emphatically illustrates Yvonne Tasker's trenchant claim that the central female characters in noir simply "do not conform in any straightforward way to conventionally feminine – that is, submissive – codes of Hollywood cinema whether by virtue of their self-interest, their sexuality, or both" (2013: 359).

56 *Improvising on the Run:* The Last Seduction

Mike's perspective is old-fashioned; he just does not understand the likes of this sexually demanding, independent woman. Desiring something akin to a conventional relationship will be a constant theme of Mike's, even as Bridget keeps him at arm's length. She will later pretend to be emotionally vulnerable, saying that she is afraid of being hurt again before sinking in the familiar femme fatale hook. Even though Bridget does not want to get close to anyone now, Mike is different: "I feel maybe I could love you." Mike soon tells Bridget that as a claim's adjuster for the insurance company, he knows a lot about people from their credit reports. He notes, for instance, that a man who recently died in a car accident was cheating on his wife. Bridget perks up.

Up until this time, the storyline is a simple theft and flight. However, armed with the knowledge that credit card records can indicate marital infidelity, Bridget begins to lay the foundation for the con game that will make Mike her partner in murder and leave him dangling for the crime. Bridget tells Mike that they are going to pitch murder to wives of such cheating men. "Your customer said she wanted her husband dead, right?" (After the fact of his accidental death). Bridget's ostensible ploy is to disclose to the wife that there is a credit card in another woman's name. The vengeful wife might then be amenable to having the cheating spouse killed and splitting the insurance money with Bridget and Mike.[1] Bridget makes a call as a test run of her fiendish offer, but lets this wife off, saying that the suggested murder is just a joke. Yet the call supposedly demonstrates to Mike that Bridget's plan is workable; however, we will discover, along with him, that it is all a ruse as part of Bridget's con to push him into getting rid of her own husband. Bridget later informs Mike that she has made the "sale" of killing another cheating husband, in Florida, but needs him to deliver on it. Mike continues to resist, telling Wendy that she is crazy. She tells Mike that she wants him to live with her in New York. When Mike insists that he will not do murder, Wendy replies, "You would if you loved me."

In the meantime, Harlan locates Bridget. The Black private eye gets in the car with her and, pointing a gun, tells her, "We want our money." Bridget makes a wisecrack about his use of the term "we," asking whether he and Clay are "an item." This homo-erotic allusion echoes an earlier scene between Harlan and Mike, and also anticipates both Bridget's subordinate con as well as the film's gruesome finale. In the earlier scene, Harlan demurred when Clay went to give him a friendly hug. In the finale, Bridget will incite Mike into "raping" her by reminding him of his upsetting marriage to a cross-dressing man, "Trish." As the scene with Harlan unfolds, Bridget badgers the private investigator into taking out his member by harping on the reputation of Black men for being well-hung (itself an encore of Mike's original wooing of Bridget). Coupled with the credit card husbands' marital infidelity and Bridget's rampant couplings with Mike, these phallic references and homo-erotic aspects of the story saturate the film in sexuality. The now genitally exposed

Improvising on the Run: The Last Seduction   57

Harlan is soon killed as Bridget slams the car into a post, herself protected by an air bag on the driver's side. Talking with a policeman at the hospital where she is recovering, Bridget explains Harlan's sexual exposure by appealing to the area's rural racism, indicating that the Black man was going to rape her with "his big…" Bridget modestly but pointedly trails off and the sympathetic officer, satisfied with Bridget's account, concludes the interview.

As with the hitting of Bridget at the story's beginning and end, penis size seems to function in the film as an indicator of inflated, and hollow, male dominance and superiority. It is so salient in the film as to acquire symbolic importance. On my interpretation, it symbolizes deluded male stature, making men even more "exposed" to already daunting female power than they might otherwise be. Even as Edmund explicitly underestimates Matty's intelligence, so do Clay, Mike, and Harlan fail to properly gauge Bridget's ability to out-maneuver them. Their manhood, literal and figurative, has infused them with a false sense of (gendered) superiority. Bridget embodies the insurmountable one-two punch of sexual control and con artist cunning. The film seems to suggest that if the resources available to the classic femme fatale are not quite enough to get the job done, then supplementing them with the wiles of a flim-flam maestro will surely be decisive. Where the classic seductress ultimately failed in her quest to get the sought-after money and be free of her husband, the talent to conceive and perpetrate a con game enables the neo-noir femme fatale to succeed, and to frame the boyfriend in the bargain!

Talking with Clay on the phone, Bridget agrees to send him the interest installment for the mobsters of $10,000 and tells him that she will return to New York after tidying up her affairs in Beston. Although she indicates to Mike that she is soon going to New York City, Bridget instead heads north, to Buffalo, the locus of Mike's abandoned marriage. When she cannot cajole, browbeat, entice, or shame Mike into going along with her murderous (but fake) insurance scam, she investigates his Buffalo sojourn and masterminds a mini-con to ensure the success of the major grift she is working on Mike. Playing a role assembled with a few scraps of information and meager props, Bridget seeks background information about Mike's whirlwind nuptials. At the County Municipal Building, she bribes a clerk to give her details of Mike's marriage, pockets a county business card, and on the way out of the building steals an office clipboard. We see Bridget introduce herself to Trish, looking for all the world like the Health Department official she pretends to be. The knowledge she gains through this short, improvised con will enable her to pressure Mike into killing an alleged violent and cheating husband in NYC. However, this is actually the major con because the victim is Clay, not a stranger with whose wife Bridget has conspired over the phone to split the insurance money.

Because insurance money is not the purpose of Bridget having her husband murdered, the story is in effect displacing the insurance fraud trope that is the

58 *Improvising on the Run:* The Last Seduction

crux of the plot of such classic noir films as *Double Indemnity* (Billy Wilder, 1944) and *The Postman Always Rings Twice* (Tay Garnett, 1946) as well as Lawrence Kasdan's more recent *Body Heat* (1981). In those earlier plots, the femme fatale manipulates her enchanted partner into killing her husband so that they can collect on his hefty insurance policy.[2] In *The Last Seduction,* Bridget displaces the fraud onto her con game, in which the husband of an abused, and cuckolded, wife is supposed to be killed for his insurance payoff. It is a con because there are, in fact, no such husbands and wives; Bridget cooks up the entire insurance narrative to pressure Mike into killing Clay.

Thinking Bridget is still out of town, a tipsy Mike calls her and records a mushy message on her answering machine. Bridget hears the message and leaves a romantic doodle on a pad for Mike to "discover" when he comes over to erase the embarrassing, lovestruck message. At her house the next morning, Mike finds ticket stubs for a trip to Miami not NYC. He is thereby manipulated into mistakenly inferring that Bridget has proceeded to kill the Florida husband. Bridget tells him that she did it for them and shows him the attache case filled with cash (from Clay's drug deal, of course). They argue and Bridget upbraids him, "You want to live bigger, but there's nothing you'd kill for. There's a place for people like that. It's called Beston." She then barks, "Get out." In her office the next day, she tells Mike that for their relationship to be between equals, he will also have to kill. She shows Mike the credit report of an unscrupulous New Yorker named Cahill. They will derive a huge payday because the insurance policy pays double for death by unnatural causes, "double indemnity." The reference to the famous film is itself doubled when Bridget later identifies herself in a phone call to the police as "Mrs. Neff" in order to detain yet another (local) private eye Clay has hired to keep tabs on her.[3] Bridget ties the money to the spurious fantasy of happily ever after: "You, me and New York City, Mike." But Mike still refuses to go along, saying, "I just realized that I don't want to be with you enough to be like you."

Bridget's Triumph

In response to Mike's continued balking at being drawn into Bridget's murderous scenario, she uses the incriminating knowledge of his aborted marriage, learned from her expedition to Buffalo, to push him into killing "Cahill" for their windfall. Bridget thereby opportunistically weaves the (Buffalo) mini-con into the dominant confidence game that she is playing on Mike. She writes a letter to Mike, supposedly from Trish, saying that she is coming to Beston to start a job at his insurance company and that, "No one has to know about our little secret" (that Mike had unwittingly married a man in drag). We do not yet know why this is such devastating news for Mike and why it immediately spurs him to tell Bridget that he will kill Cahill, never to return to

Improvising on the Run: The Last Seduction   59

Beston. For all his genital grandeur, then, Mike is sexually insecure enough to wish to flee the perceived arrival of his former (Trans) love interest.

We learn with Mike that "Cahill" is actually Clay, Bridget's husband. As Mike pokes the sleeping spouse with a gun, saying that he is "here to rob him," Clay wittily quips, "I thought you were the new decorator." More nervous than Clay, Mike has the husband handcuff himself to a chair and gag himself. Attempting to stab Clay, Mike moans, "I can't do it Wendy. I can't do it." Clay immediately grasps that Mike is Bridget's henchman, remembering that she is using "Wendy" as her fake name and hops over to their wedding photo to demonstrate the truth to Mike. Clay tells Mike that Wendy/Bridget is his wife and explains about the money. Intuiting the romantic entanglement, Clay presciently explains that after killing him, Bridget will finger Mike for the murder.

Outside, Bridget sees that the lights of the apartment have been turned back on, signaling that Mike has supposedly done away with Clay. When she enters the apartment, however, Mike says, "So you were gonna have me kill your husband." Bridget acknowledges the truth of this but denies that she was going to turn him into the police. Clay interjects, "Bullshit." Surmising that Bridget would cast Mike in the role of the jealous boyfriend in the frame-up for the police, Clay adds, "I guess Mikey wasn't up to it." At this point, we do not know how the situation is going to play out, but we do know how Bridget has conned Mike into his murderous role. She paces, considering her options and Clay asks her if she wants to stay married. Bridget bends down to kiss the supine Clay, who is still handcuffed on the couch, but instead decisively sprays mace into his mouth, killing him.

Mike jumps in, pulls Bridget off Clay, and while he fumbles with the limp body, Bridget wipes her prints off the cannister of mace. She says, "Now we have a future." Mike wails, "You're not human." Bridget coolly proceeds to insert the fruits of her subsidiary, Buffalo con, telling Mike, "Trish wasn't really coming to Beston, Mike." She taunts him for marrying a man in drag and Mike hits her a couple of times, echoing Clay's initial slapping of Bridget: the outward display of male dominance, but behavior that is actually flailing. Bridget then goads Mike into "raping" her as if she were a stand-in for Trish. Enraged, Mike does not register that Bridget has dialed the police and that they hear Mike braying, for the benefit of the police operator, that he had indeed killed her husband.

As with Ned, we soon see Mike in prison, talking with a lawyer. The lawyer informs him that the Miami man Bridget allegedly killed does indeed exist, but is very much alive. Just another patch of Bridget's well-stitched grifter's quilt. He tells Mike that the case looks bleak, but Mike comes up with "one thing" that will exonerate him. Cut to Bridget in a chauffeured limousine. She is burning the "one thing:" the apartment identification slip with the name "Cahill" on it that she had inserted in place of "Gregory," her

60 *Improvising on the Run:* The Last Seduction

married name, to trick Mike into killing her husband. Driving away in New York splendor parallels Matty reclining on a sun-soaked beach. Both women have managed to indict their would-be male paramours for their crimes, the lethal "blow off" for a winning con. At films' end, Matty and Bridget are now free to enjoy the spoils that memorable femmes fatales typically are denied.

In an understated way, these neo-noir films inflate the moral ambiguity that permeates classical noir by revamping the character of the murdered husband. In the canonical movies, such as *Double Indemnity* and *The Postman Always Rings Twice*, the husband is no worse than boring, old, or in the way. The murderess chafes in a stultifying marriage and is desperate for a way out, preferably well-heeled. However, in our neo-noir film-stories, the husband is cast in a morally culpable light. The despised spouse is now himself criminal – Edmund in *Body Heat,* or illicit – Clay in *The Last Seduction.* The eliminated men are themselves morally shady and this makes the moral landscape of these movies a bit murky. Although the femmes fatales are bad, the immorality of the husbands mitigates their wickedness just enough to create a small emotional-moral space in which we can appreciate the full array of their impressive abilities.

The pair of films examined here represent a synthesis of the femme fatale narrative and the con caper. Both seductive women do away with their spouses and keep all the contested money. They operate within the familiar film noir triangular structure; however, where Phyllis Dietrich (*Double Indemnity)* and Cora Smith (*The Postman Always Rings Twice)* fail, Matty and Bridget succeed. They are neither killed nor jailed, but make off with the substantial haul. The neo-noir movies revise the classical storyline by virtue of the superior intelligence and gumption of their femmes fatales. The vixens succeed because they fold clever con games into the old-fashioned playing on male desire and fantasy. Matty has had the luxury of building her complex con game over an extended period of time: getting the lowdown on Ned's clunky legal career; learning the details of Florida law with regard to botched wills; paying off the real Matty Tyler in order to assume her name or identity. On the other hand, Bridget has had to improvise her flimflam while on the run from Clay: using Mike's insider knowledge to construct a believable scheme that will actually serve as her encompassing grift and then piecing together the truth about Mike's bizarre and humiliating marriage in order to stage a nested con game, also conjured on the spot. Where Matty weaves her mug smoothly into her well-thought-out scam, Bridget has to shove her lover into her spontaneously hatched con. The effect of enriching the femme fatale's treacherous tango with a con game is that the beguiling protagonists are endowed with the new, powerful dimension of crafty intelligence. The erotic package conceals a brilliant mind, yielding an indomitable sorceress.

Notes

1 The cheating husband nicely mirrors the infidelity of both Matty and Bridget, although the unfaithfulness of the femmes fatales includes murder

2 *Body Heat* can be viewed as a variant on this plot device. In this film-story, a fraudulent will replaces the insurance policy as the instrument whereby the murderous wife is to collect her husband's estate, although there is likely insurance payout for Matty as well

3 Recall that Walter Neff (Fred MacMurray) is the insurance salesman who falls under Phyllis Dietrichson's spell in *Double Indemnity.*

Bibliography

Aristotle (1962). *Nicomachean Ethics,* trans. Martin Ostwald. Indianapolis, IN: Bobbs-Merrill.

Brookes, Ian (2017). *Film Noir: A Critical Introduction.* London: Bloomsbury.

Foot, Philippa (1993). "Virtues and Vices." In *Vice and Virtue in Everyday Life.* Eds. Christina and Fred Sommers. Orlando, FL: Harcourt, Brace, Jovanovich, 2nd ed., 216–231.

Godlovitch, Stanley (1993). "On Wisdom." In *Vice and Virtue in Everyday Life,* Eds. Christina and Fred Sommers. Orlando, FL: Harcourt, Brace, Jovanovich, 2nd ed., 262–284.

Tasker, Yvonne (2013). "Women in Film Noir." In *A Companion to Film Noir.* Eds. Andrea Spicer and Helen Hanso. Oxford: Blackwell, 353 – 368.

Filmography

Dahl, John (1994). *The Last Seduction.* UK.

Garnett, Tay (1946). *The Postman Always Rings Twice.* U.S.

Kasdan, Lawrence (1981). *Body Heat.* U.S.

Maxwell, Ronald (1993). *Gettysburg.* U.S.

Wilder, Billy (1944). *Double Indemnity.* U.S.

5 Con Game as Prelude to Love

Birthday Girl

Looking for Love

Jez Butterworth's 2001 film opens with a young British man looking into the camera that is recording his message for prospective Russian brides on the website "From Russia with Love." He is pleasant-looking but not handsome. John Buckingham (Ben Chaplin) is nervous and has to start over. He enumerates his interests or tastes: "Running, reading, going out, staying in…" He is looking for someone who is intelligent and kind, and although pretty would be nice it is not critical. Facing the camera establishes a kind of intimacy with us in the audience. The ongoing voice-over reinforces our identification with him and his status as the principal figure in the narrative. As Eric Smoodin argues, "Once the presence of the voice-over narrator has been established, the entire film serves as a sort of linguistic event, as the narrator's speech" (1983: 19). Consequently, even when John stops narrating through voice-over, we view the story as about him as well as from him.

In his voice-over, John explains how difficult it is to meet someone. He rationalizes his pursuit of a long-distance, foreign-born bride. He notes that some people would not understand what he is doing and find it a bit sad, but he claims that it is a "brave, reasonable thing to do." Is he justifying himself to the audience or to himself? As he is still looking into the camera, it is plausible to hear the justification as part of his spiel to potential mates. John feels the need to explain himself as part of his recorded profile. He even notes the chronic ant problem in his home, perhaps inadvertently signifying the smallness of his life and its problems. His work as a mid-tier officer in a regional bank reinforces the dull, plodding quality of his daily routines. The arrival of the woman John chooses will certainly liven up his erstwhile hive-like existence, but not in the way he hopes. Although Nadia (Nicole Kidman) is beautiful, she is not quite as advertised. Her apparent lack of English competency dismays John as he explicitly wants "someone you can really talk to." But that is merely the most glaring discrepancy between what John expects and the reality of his Russian amour. Nadia is, in fact, a con-artist, in league with two male, Slavic cohorts. We, in the audience, discover this along with John,

DOI: 10.4324/9781003364542-6

Con Game as Prelude to Love: Birthday Girl   63

at the same time the trio makes clear that they have been playing him in order to make off with money from the bank at which he joylessly toils.

The film deftly departs from typical con game movies in several ways. Most cinematic con artists are men. In this film, although a woman has male accomplices, she is central to the grift. As with *Body Heat* and *The Last Seduction*, in which women are the (atypical) perpetrators of the con game, Nadia uses her erotic charms to entrap her mark. But where Matty and Bridget in the former movies are not professional con artists, aiming for one big killing through the murder of their husbands, Nadia is indeed a professional con artist. Rather than ensnare her dupe to rid her of an unwanted spouse, Nadia entrances John with the promise of making him her husband: a reversal of the famous *noir* plot. She and her Russian buddies have worked the same scam on a line of lonely men before John. Unlike most con game films, *Birthday Girl* includes physical coercion and actual violence, in addition to feigned mayhem. The con artists in cinema tend to take pride in eschewing the crudeness of actual violence, favoring the illusion of physical coercion over its actual deployment. Perhaps most unusual, this film situates the revelation of the flimflam considerably before the ending of the story. This then leaves room for further complications and surprises.

The central complication and surprise is the way the interaction between John and Nadia evolves into a genuine romantic friendship. John's outrage at being played for a chump, along with the destruction of his banking career, gradually gives way to affection and support for Nadia, whom he views as being ill-treated by the more aggressive of her Russian confederates. The upshot is a sweeping irony. John was naively looking for a "mail-order" bride through the Internet and his naivete left him prey to the con artists' ploy. The illusion of romance was further fostered by erotic play on Nadia's part. The developing of a genuine emotional attachment that ensues after the disclosure of the con game is, then, ironic: falling victim to a con game as a result of seeking marital happiness results in the beginning of a truly loving connection. The con of a romantic relationship, then, lays the groundwork for an incipient, honest bond.

How does the energetic antipathy between John and Nadia morph into shared attraction? The feelings between John and Nadia deepen as a result of a radical change in their speech and action. Nadia had obviously deceived John by pretending not to understand English. So, from the beginning, their verbal interaction is stunted. But it is further distorted by the limited way John presents himself, both on the taped overture through the phony marital website, "From Russia with Love," and by what he cannot convey in person to the supposedly linguistically challenged Nadia. But once the con is disclosed, Nadia demonstrates total proficiency in English and the verbal gloves come off. Each criticizes the other in stringent but truthful terms. Nadia makes fun of John presuming to find true love through a website and John, rightfully, accuses Nadia of prostituting herself. After all, she has been having sex with

64   *Con Game as Prelude to Love:* Birthday Girl

a string of dupes, culminating in John, as ingredient to the con game that she runs with her Russian buddies. Their lacerating mutual criticism is, after all, on the mark, as if flaying away the pretense of their website portraits and Nadia's in-person play-acting. Their verbal attacks expose John and Nadia to one another, while also promoting self-reflection. Punctuated by angry slapping, the spoken exchanges actually propel them into a greater understanding of one another as well as themselves.

The arguments and criticisms are framed by serious, existential conditions on each side. For John, the theft of bank monies apparently destroys his career, however dull and stultifying it had been slogging along. For her part, Nadia is carrying on, and throwing up, while pregnant. Moreover, the child is not welcomed by Alexei, the con artist with whom Nadia had been sexually involved. Consequently, John and Nadia both anticipate futures that are not only uncertain but problematic. Besides the penetrating of veneers that their verbal fighting facilitates, the pair collaborate to solve problems. Helping one another and working together promote their understanding and appreciation for one another. First, there is the satisfaction of cooperating and achieving a successful outcome. Hiding John's car, evading the police, wresting the stolen money from Alexei, and, finally, making it onto an airplane to a new life. During their trials and exertions, the pair witness and appreciate each other's effort and ability to navigate their imperiled journey. Along with the searing criticisms and comments they exchange, the shared labors in extricating themselves from British law and Russian collusion also deepen their growing knowledge of each other. In addition, during their teamwork, they unexpectedly bring out the best in one another. Seeing John risk himself for her, spurs Nadia to ingenuity and daring. Watching Nadia defy her former lover motivates John to take on a ruthless antagonist and also jettison his career for the sake of Nadia and her child. A basis has been laid for a real romantic attachment, more solid than the casual and artificial interaction that had preceded it.

The sexual delight that Nadia had been providing John, and that mitigated his disappointment in not having a companion with whom to converse, was hardly the substance of real romantic love, *eros*. C.S. Lewis succinctly captures the difference between sexual love and lust: "Without Eros [romantic love] sexual desire, like every other desire, is a fact about ourselves. Within Eros it is rather about the Beloved" (1960: 13). Without care for and about the other person, sexual interaction is on a par with the shallow profiles exchanged on the Russian website. It trades in appearances and immediate sensations. Real love requires knowledge of the other person and delight in the ever-expanding awareness of who they truly are. In romantic love, sexual desire is instigated by loving the other; we seek erotic interaction in order to experience the other more completely and to reveal ourselves more fully. The beauty of *Birthday Girl* is found in the way a con game story gradually bends its tone and direction into an arc of genuinely amorous affection. The

Con Game as Prelude to Love: Birthday Girl   65

role-playing and deceptions that are the "substance" of con games, including the pretenses exhibited by the mark himself, are shown being penetrated by truthful speech and cooperative interaction. The speech and interaction enable John and Nadia to finally see one another, and themselves, for who they truly are. The upshot is a willingness to venture forth together, into a future that is uncertain and definitely risky, but promising.

Complementing the shift in tone and meaning is a story that keeps us off-balance. Elements of slapstick, humorous dialogue, and unexpected discoveries create a playful ambience. For example, we see John running across a parking lot with guitar cases filled with money, hear Nadia assent in English to being a giraffe, and watch Nadia find a bag of John's kinky pornographic magazines. But these lighthearted episodes alternate with scenes of physical assault and threats of actual bodily harm. The shifts in mood prepare us for the unexpected, hopeful conclusion. The film is buttressed by numerous parallels and repetitions, including its opening and closing scenes at the airport.

Getting Acquainted

At the airport, we watch John anxiously await and look for the woman he has chosen over the Internet. After all the passengers have apparently departed, he sees a tall, willowy woman standing shyly apart, beautiful but heavily made-up. Riding home, John discovers to his dismay that Nadia seems to know almost no English as she responds "yes," to everything he says, including "Are you a giraffe?" We will learn along with John, much later, that Nadia is actually fluent in English. Feigning ignorance of his language is part of Nadia's ruse. Nadia smokes, then vomits out the car window and then by the side of the road, symptomatic of her, hitherto undetected, pregnancy. John makes a series of calls to the matchmaking organization, increasingly desperate, to renege on the arrangement as Nadia apparently lacks the linguistic proficiency that was advertised and that John values so highly. No one answers the phone and the calls are never returned. We will later surmise that the website and the organization behind it are the phony front of the con game. At dinner, Nadia forcefully insists that John put on the ring she proffers. Nadia's appearance in his bedroom startles John. He jumps out of bed and backs away from her. Nadia guides his hand to her breast, puts one hand on his mouth and with the other strokes his genitals until he climaxes. She exits his room as their relationship has taken an erotic, though linguistically challenged, turn. She will soon up the ante and mount him during sex in order to forestall his announced booking of a flight for her return to Russia.

Each tries surreptitiously to learn more about the other. While Nadia is in the shower, John rifles through her suitcase, perusing childhood pictures of her and a pair of binoculars. For her part, Nadia goes through John's personal affects, unearthing a plastic bag filled with magazines of sado-masochistic pornography. The opportunity presents itself during John's day at the bank at

66 *Con Game as Prelude to Love:* Birthday Girl

which he works. His voice-over is now morphed into John giving his yearly report, which, in turn, elicits his supervisor's assessment of his work. It is totally bland: "John makes able decisions in most areas of his job." John receives no promotion but is given keys to the vault, central to the con game about to be played on him. John's boss drones on in the most pedestrian evaluation, "A sound, workmanlike year." John acquiesces in a milquetoast manner, "Thank you. I think that's very fair." Because his response to the grift Nadia and her cohorts spring on him both enlivens his drab existence and evokes his courage, we view it as something of a tonic to his dead-end job and ant-infested house. Upon returning home, John gives Nadia a Russian-English dictionary as a gift, to which she responds by placing his porn magazines on the table, including "Hog-Tied Bitches." She will soon accommodate his sexual taste by making binding gestures with his tie. The humor does not disguise the fact that, after all, Nadia is in charge.

Back at the bank, John participates in a sensitivity training session which involves the individual falling backward and being caught by his colleagues. It is called, "Trust and Letting Go." This is what John will do at the film's finale. He will let go of the stifling safety of his old life and trust Nadia to be his partner in an unknown future. The somewhat jocular scene of the training session, then, will resonate meaningfully with John's climactic existential decision. Meanwhile, the couple seems to be settling into a comfortable rhythm, albeit one in which sexual adventure provides the emphatic beat. We watch them walking in a lovely wood near a pond as well as strolling through town. We also see John binding Nadia's hands to the bedpost preparatory to their sexual adventure. When not using her needles to knit a sweater, Nadia pushes them into John's chest as part of their erotic play. But all this is about to change dramatically.

Birthday Party, Russian Style

Continuing to knit a red sweater and swat the ubiquitous ants with her dictionary, Nadia announces that her birthday is today. John is soon taken aback at the boisterous arrival of two Russian men who have come to celebrate Nadia's birthday. We wonder how the pair knew where Nadia was staying in England. Brandishing and swigging vodka, the two men take over the celebration, loud and vivacious. Yuri (Mathieu Kassovitz) is Nadia's friend. He explains to John that they are actors, and Alexei (Vincent Cassel) is a guitarist who (purportedly) does not speak English and whom Yuri has recently met. They show John their passports in response to John's inquiring into their plans and legitimacy. Yuri seems charming: friendly, enthusiastic, and helpful. He suggests that John say something to Nadia in English and he will translate it for her. After affirming her liking of England, Nadia tells Yuri that she has a secret to tell John. She had watched John at the airport, using her father's binoculars, taking her father's advice about sizing people up from afar.

Con Game as Prelude to Love: Birthday Girl   **67**

The binoculars will take on symbolic meaning as the story unfolds. They enable Nadia and John to see one another as they truly are. In the advertising and con game on the part of Nadia there is deception but John also presents and conceals himself to suit his interests. The film suggests that looking at each other from a distance, yet brought into focus by the binoculars, is a departure from their everyday perception. John will also use the binoculars to alert Nadia to his presence near the airport and Alexei will rightly interpret the binocular story along with Nadia's father's role in it as indicative of her genuine affection for John. The film segues from Nadia describing taking a mental picture of John at the airport through the binoculars to Yuri taking a Polaroid photo of John, Nadia, and Alexei. A birthday memento.

The next morning, while John is out on his morning jog through the woods, we get a foreshadowing of Alexei as a menacing presence. He catches up to John, prods him, and invites him to shadow box. Alexei then spins and athletically elevates to kick the branch of a tree. His action is at once playful and threatening. In the bathroom at work, John peruses his own Russian-English dictionary and composes a note to Nadia in Russian. She will unearth it much later in the glove compartment of John's car and she will find it moving: both what it says and the effort John made to create it for her. The heartfelt note will augment the development of their relationship that painful but candid conversations encourage.

The four of them soon frolic in the neighboring pond: jumping, splashing, and dunking one another. But again, Alexei seems dangerous. John sees him get too frisky with Nadia. Nadia scolds him but then the two of them disappear underwater. John submerges himself in order to see what is going on but to no avail: a telling image of his inability to perceive their long-standing, familiar relationship. John then protests when Alexei holds Nadia underwater. Nadia remonstrates with Alexei and Yuri comes over to tell him to leave Nadia alone. Nadia leaves, apparently in a huff. Alexei is intentionally setting himself up as the bad guy for the purpose of the con game, and yet his play-acting bespeaks his real nature. Even when not playing a role, Alexei is easily angered and physically rough. As a result of Alexei's disturbing behavior, John tells him and Yuri that they must leave. Yuri apologizes and John indicates that he is not the cause of their eviction. Yuri deceptively explains that he does not know Alexei well and that perhaps he should have come alone. Alexei pretends ignorance of the conversation but in the morning, he accosts John for throwing him out. He takes out a knife and has Nadia bound and gagged. In Russian, Alexei says, "You think you're better than me." He throws a protesting Yuri down and threatens to douse Nadia with a kettle of hot water. Alexei demands that John go to the bank to get money or he will hurt Nadia. Rather than threaten John, the con game turns on endangering the woman with whom the con artists have entangled John.

The film started out as a quirky romantic comedy, but with Alexei's aggressiveness it swerves. Nadia's knitting and vomiting suggest that she

68   *Con Game as Prelude to Love:* Birthday Girl

is pregnant and John's robbing the bank adds to the serious shadow that is cast on the proceedings. Wielding two empty guitar cases, John returns to the bank, deflecting various coworkers' request that he play something on the guitars he seems to be toting. A visiting officer is being shown around the bank, witnessing another session of "Trust and Letting Go." During the palaver that accompanies the administrator's visit, John opens the vault with his newly acquired key, and stuffs the guitar cases with the bank's holdings. The farcical aspect of his theft is heightened by a long shot of John running from the bank across the parking lot with the now-engorged guitar cases.

Con Game Revealed

Cut to John driving his car after the robbery, with his three Russians passengers. When John sees Nadia and Alexei canoodling in the back seat, he realizes that Nadia is not a prisoner after all, and the con is exposed. Tying her up and threatening her unless John brought money from the bank was a scam, beginning with the "From Russia with Love" website communication. In a motel, the Russians count their haul and rejoice at its size – over $90,000. The scene is flavored with mirth as Yuri quibbles with Alexei over the money he spent on various things, including tickets for the Broadway show "Cats." Nadia asks about the show and is told that everything about the set was large, so you, in the audience, felt cat-size. But the genial air is soon dispelled by Alexei's hostility. He brusquely interrogates Nadia about the quantity of sex she had with John. She is put off and does not answer. In the bathroom, Yuri asks John how he is doing. Not great, as John is gagged and bound to the toilet in his underpants. Yuri shows John photos of other marks to make him feel less bad (perhaps for his gullibility). Yuri tells John that he was the best of the lot, but in what sense? Most affable or least trouble? Yuri seems solicitous, even sympathetic, thanking John and apologetically taking the ring from John's finger, no doubt for future use with another unsuspecting sucker in search of love in Russian places.

In the bedroom, Nadia asks Alexei if they can finally stop (their trickster ways). Nadia says that she wants to call it quits. Angered once again, Alexei remarks on the rope burns on Nadia's wrists which Nadia tries to explain away as cooking mishaps. Alexei expresses his irritation over Nadia's charming story of watching John through her father's binoculars at the airport. He demands to know if the yarn is true, suspicious that Nadia has some real affection for John. In an effort to placate Alexei, Nadia gives him the red sweater she had been knitting. As Alexei kisses her, Nadia confides that she is pregnant. She points out that her chronic upchucking corroborates that the baby is indeed his. But Alexei is not enthusiastic about impending parenthood; he sees the child as a burden and an impediment to their grifting ways. He goes into the bathroom, gazes first at himself in the mirror then at John and takes another swig from a bottle of vodka.

Con Game as Prelude to Love: Birthday Girl   69

After a short take of a throng of people and police outside John's house, discussing his larceny, we watch John wriggle out of his bonds and get dressed. In the adjacent room, Nadia is also bound and her mouth taped. Apparently, Alexei has directed his ire at his girlfriend as well. John unties Nadia and eagerly rips off the tape on her mouth, forcibly and painfully. Nadia gasps and John slaps her. She wallops him and they tussle. They pummel each other on the bed, quasi-erotically. John pins Nadia's hands, holding her down with his body and legs, facing him, reprising their former sado-masochistic hijinks. Nadia knees him in the groin and he rolls off the bed, onto the floor, groaning. On her back, Nadia pants, as if in post-coital exhaustion. John jerks on the bedspread, as if it were a tablecloth, dumping Nadia on the floor. She blurts, "Great. You split my fucking lip." John is flabbergasted to learn that Nadia speaks flawless, colloquial English.

In the following scene, the pair are sitting in a restaurant, where Nadia explains that the con artists have found that the sham of linguistic ignorance makes their plans go more smoothly. She then tries to placate the numb and silent John, saying that the bank will not blame him and that he can get his life back. But she smiles and adds, "I bet you hated the bank," as if actually doing him a favor. When John responds by calling her a prostitute, Nadia slaps him. He slaps her back and they start wrangling again. Interrupted by the waitress, John asks where the nearest police station is. He smirks and chuckles as a flustered Nadia tells him that she needs his help. When Nadia acknowledges John's desire to punish her, to be vindictive, he archly (and sarcastically) rejoins, "In every sense. If at all possible." Pleading her case, Nadia says that John cannot hurt her more than she's been hurt already. Continuing in his facetious vein, John assures her, "If it's all the same to you, I'd like to give it a bash."

Nadia sighs and says that her name is not "Nadia," but does not disclose her real name, yet. This simple truth is precious and the film employs names as an understated trope for knowledge of an individual's true identity. In the car, John scoffs at Nadia's sob story about how hard it is for women in Russia to get decent jobs. He intones, "It's so cold [in Russia] we have to go to England and shag people to get warm!" He continues to have a bit of spiteful fun at Nadia's expense. But once in the police station, John cottons to Nadia's pregnancy as he hears her throwing up in the bathroom. Knowledge of her condition softens him and he relents, leaving the police station without turning her in. Back in the car, the duo hears of John's escapade on the radio and that he is known to be driving an orange car. He ascertains that Nadia's flight home is the next day. Nadia tells John that she appreciates him sparing her, adding with unintended humor, "I'm sorry that you're a fugitive from justice."

What ensues is a cutting exchange, but one that, perhaps ironically, encourages interpersonal (but non-sexual) intimacy. Their accusations and recriminations slice away at the pretense and facades that have shaped their preceding interactions. John is still angry and asks "Nadia" whether when she

70   *Con Game as Prelude to Love:* Birthday Girl

was a little girl did she plan on having sex with many men, "Stealing their homes, jobs and dignity." Nadia retorts, "Did you want to still be in this town, with a job I hate, a house full of ants, and a big bag of pornography?" She pushes further into John's artifice and fantasy, asking rhetorically whether he really expected a Russian wife to fall in love with him. John abruptly pulls the car off the road and sits under a tree, in a sulk. Nadia rightly points out that the police are looking for his (distinctively colored) car, adding, "This is not a very good plan."

Reacquaintance and Fresh Turmoil

Rummaging for snacks in the car's glove compartment, Nadia discovers the note John composed in Russian for her. Consulting his own Russian-English dictionary, John managed this: "Dear Nadia. You are only girl in world. I dream to talk. What will happen?" Nadia is touched by the sentiments expressed and the effort John has made to communicate with her in her own language, back when he thought she did not know English. The note augments the impact of John reversing his vengeful course due to Nadia's pregnancy and the barbed but honest criticisms they have hurled at each other; we sense that the relationship between the two of them is growing into something more emotionally fulfilling. They push the car off the road, into the trees and start walking through the woods toward the airport. When they finally stop for the night, Nadia jocularly points her gun-shaped cigarette lighter at John and then uses it to build a fire.

In an effort to learn more about John, Nadia probes his relationship with a former girlfriend. She had found a photo of a blonde woman, "The short one with small eyes." John retorts that their relationship is none of her business and that the woman did not have small eyes. Nadia persists, asking whether the woman left him. Nadia jests, asking whether the woman left John for her boss or John's best friend (scenarios familiar to Nadia from popular culture). John snaps, "She's dead!" Nadia gasps and apologizes. John stammers, "I... don't know why I said that." To which Nadia joyfully exclaims, "She's alive? She's alive!" A chastened John grumbles, "Laugh it up." Despite the goofiness of the exchange and the fact that it really does not go anywhere, failing to round out Nadia's knowledge of John's life, the incident does expand the range of their conversation. Alone and with nothing pressing for them to do, the couple have the leisure to explore each other's history. Nadia asks again why John's relationship with "small eyes" ended. He replies that he does not know. When Nadia asks for the woman's name, John simply says, "What's your name?" Recall that Nadia had told John that "Nadia" was not her real name but does not provide it now, as if sharing this truth about herself is too intimate and, then again, John has not given her the name of his former girlfriend.

Although names do not seem obviously self-disclosing, the film is offering them as significant, intimating that for Nadia and John names are emblematic

Con Game as Prelude to Love: Birthday Girl 71

of identity. In asking for names, John and Nadia are in effect asking, "Who are you, really?" Even though Nadia does know John's name, the name of his old flame would reflect on his identity. As the ignorance of names carries the admission that neither truly knows who the other person is, it actually represents a deepening of their mutual understanding. It is the calm, constructive complement of their earlier biting attack: each dimension candidly pushing their relationship past appearances or the immediate delights of sex into the uncharted waters of personal identification and revelation. In addition, Nadia has been wearing less and less eye makeup as the story progresses, uncovering more of her natural self and its beauty.

After sleeping in the rough, the pair resumes walking, down roads and across fields. In the evening, they arrive at the airport. John tells Nadia that he has to leave. Nadia asks him what he is going to do and John says, "Uh... I don't know." She gives John the binoculars as a parting gift, smiles shyly and says goodbye. John leaves and Nadia looks after him with misgiving, distraught at the predicament in which she has left him. John approaches police outside the airport terminal to turn himself in, but must wait while they deal with another person. In the interim, John looks through the binoculars and sees Alexei sitting next to Nadia, with Yuri standing nearby. Reversing Nadia's story of watching John at the airport through her father's binoculars, John is now watching Nadia and her cohorts, at the airport and through the binoculars. The ability to see closely yet at a distance seems symbolic: distance with granular vision puts things in their proper perspective. As if we need a technological mediation of our vision in order to see reality accurately; in contrast with the technological mediation of the Internet profiles that obscured or distorted perception of what was real about both John and Nadia. Alexei is rough with Nadia, hauls her to her feet and marches her out of the airport. John puts his athletic training to good use, running after the cab that is taking the trio to a nearby motel. Why is he pursuing the Russians? To "save" Nadia? We may guess that John does not himself know why he follows them, except perhaps that he is impelled by some vague concern for Nadia's safety, given Alexei's temperament and his brutish behavior at the airport.

John looks in through a window from outside the motel and sees Alexei arranging the money in their room. We continue to watch from John's vantage point as Alexei tries to kiss Nadia. At first, she turns away and then, after they do kiss, she goes into another room looking frantically for something. Alexei again manhandles Nadia. A motel worker delivers the binoculars that John had earlier passed along in an effort to learn which room the Russians were occupying. Nadia registers the presence of the binoculars with alarm, realizing that John must be nearby. The subversive significance of the eyepiece ripples. Alexei pushes Nadia to the bed, provoked by the appearance of the binoculars. He immediately grasps their importance, in the moment, and more generally as symbolizing the bond between Nadia and the British mark. John gasps, "Oh, Jesus," and crawls in through the bathroom window. Meanwhile,

72 *Con Game as Prelude to Love:* Birthday Girl

Alexei demands of Nadia, "So you came back here just to rob me?" But he quickly backs off, saying that now the two of them are even since earlier he had panicked over learning of the baby: "I'm sorry... we're square." But Nadia recoils as Alexei tries to kiss her.

Having crept into the room, John attempts a ruse of his own. He brandishes Nadia's gun-lighter in order to intimidate Alexei, but the ploy "backfires" as Alexei had, in fact, given the lighter to Nadia and so cannot be fooled. He mocks John's vain maneuver and cheerfully thumps him. Nadia implores, "Don't hurt him!" Alexei asks, "What do you care?" and Nadia rejoins, "He came here with me." Alexei rightly surmises that Nadia and John are some-how complicit, "I knew something was going on [between the two of you]." Nadia retorts, "You don't know anything and you don't own me." The claim about ownership, however, does seem to confirm Alexei's suspicions. Why say, "You don't own me," unless you are asserting your freedom from an individual, and with it also the freedom to be involved with someone else. Alexei pulls out a knife, holds it under John's throat and snarls: "If you love him so much, let's see you do it [make love]." Nadia begs Alexei to stop what he is doing. John looks on, wide-eyed in terror and Nadia obeys Alexei and kisses John. There is genuine passion or affection in her kiss and this seems to amaze John.

Alexei slumps in a chair, convinced that Nadia does indeed care for John; however, he soon regains his animus and flings John to the floor before pounc-ing on Nadia on the bed. In preparation to assaulting her, Alexei groans, "You hate me and I showed you the world." Whereupon, John whacks Alexei from behind with a guitar and the pair then gives the volatile Russian a taste of his own medicine; they tie him up and tape his mouth shut. Nadia indicates that the stolen money is secreted in Alexei's coat, which they take. On the way out of the motel, they slip by Yuri, who is absorbed playing an electronic game in the motel's lobby.

A New Beginning

At the airport, Nadia and John hear the call for passengers to proceed to the gate for the Moscow flight. They say goodbye to one another. John asks Nadia what she will do. Echoing John's earlier reply to the same question, she says, "I don't know. Something else [other than sexualized con games]." When John asks, "Promise?" she reassuringly adds, "Promise." John says good-bye again. Looking beautiful and vulnerable, Nadia kisses John tenderly on the lips. They smooch a bit more. Nadia takes off Alexei's coat, saying that she does not want it (stuffed with money). John magnanimously tells her to spend it on the baby, when he could most likely return the purloined funds to the bank, explain himself, and wriggle free from legal entanglement. Where Alexei wants nothing to do with his own child, John is willing to forfeit his own future for its welfare with Nadia. Moreover, during their sojourn in the

Con Game as Prelude to Love: Birthday Girl   73

forest, John chided Nadia for smoking while pregnant. His solicitousness contrasts dramatically with Alexei's distaste at the prospect of fatherhood and rough treatment of his pregnant girlfriend. John is clearly identifying with Nadia and her future. Although he is not experiencing full-blown love, he is taking the caring point of view that is essential to it. Shulamith Firestone lyrically expresses this as looking through an extra window on the world, "each enlarging himself through the other" (1989: 30). We identify with the beloved's interests and desires, "as if... [he or she] were a part of ourselves" (Peck, 1978: 117). Nadia appreciates John's caring identification with her, realizing that it is totally foreign to Alexei.

In Russian, Nadia says, "You're always surprising me." John jests, "You know, when I said that I didn't speak Russian, I wasn't just making that up." Nadia whispers something to him. John stares at her and she bites her lip coquettishly. John wryly notes, "It's a long way to go for a date [referring to Moscow]." In a breathless coo, Nadia says, "I know," and hands John Alexei's ticket and passport. She had filched them back in the motel in the hopes that John could take Alexei's place, on the plane and in her life. John tells Nadia that he does not know her and she replies, "I don't know you, either." But they know enough to be drawn to each other. Through their shared ordeal, looking out for one another, and their cutting, mutual criticism, the Brit and Russian have actually begun an open relationship in which they do reveal themselves. They have gained an appreciation of who they really are instead of responding to the various subterfuges and facades that had characterized their former interaction. Even as John and Nadia are gaining knowledge of the other, so are they increasing their self-awareness. For example, John is forced to acknowledge that he does not like his work at the bank very much and Nadia has to face the fact that performing in the series of con games does involve her prostituting herself. Along the way, she also sees how violent Alexei is and that he has no interest in a domestic life with her and their child. Even so, going to Russia with Nadia is a huge leap, including a leap of faith. Recall the sensitivity training at the bank: "Trust and Letting Go." John will have to trust Nadia, and his own fragile judgment about the two of them as a couple, and let go: of his career, his old life, his very country.

While John and Nadia prepare to get on their Russian-bound flight, Yuri returns to the room and sees the remnants of the struggle as well as the furious, bound Alexei. They jump in a taxi, Alexei commanding, "Airport!" Upon arriving at the airport, he will get the unpleasant surprise that his passport and ticket are missing. The film then has recourse to the well-worn device of "race-against-time." Can Nadia and John escape before Yuri and Alexei corral them? On line at the airport, John dons the lucre-laden leather coat of Alexei's, in order to look more authentically Russian. Nadia instructs him to say "da" ("yes") to whatever question she puts to him in Russian, which will supposedly evidence John's Slavic bona fides. Nadia asks John in Russian if he is OK; he dutifully replies, "Da." He repeats his monosyllabic answer

74 *Con Game as Prelude to Love:* Birthday Girl

when she asks if he is a giraffe. To the British official, not knowing Russian, the exchange should sound plausible. The conversation also serves to distract the airport official since John does not look much like the picture of Alexei on the passport.

John's repetition of "da" comically but tellingly mirrors Nadia's opening stream of "yes" to the questions John had put to her in the car after collecting her at the airport. Nadia's feigning of English deficiency is paralleled by John's masquerade of Russian proficiency, only now John and Nadia are in cahoots, neither seeking to fool the other. The deeper meaning is that John's actions are taken to realize a genuine commitment (to Russia), however nascent; whereas, Nadia's pretense was in the service of a phony commitment (to England). Where John mistakenly thought he was acquiring a Russian bride, Nadia's deception of the authorities at the airport is designed to bring her a potential British groom.

Yuri and Alexei are too late to prevent the couple from taking flight. Passing through the metal detector, John places the symbolic binoculars on the tray, underscoring their role in his current arrangement. As they walk to the plane, Nadia confides, "My name is Sophia," as if sharing the most intimate of details. As noted, the film elevates names to just that, a trope of accurate and important personal information. John has not lost his sense of irony and responds, "Well Sophia, mine's still John." Sophia says, "Hello John." She is codifying their reacquaintance for their new life abroad. As they are carried along a moving walkway (a mini-prelude to being transported through the air to a new continent), they look at each other. They bestow soft smiles on one another as they both turn forward, looking toward their uncertain but promising future.

The overarching form of the story is one of irony. A lonely young British man seeks a foreign-born mate through the Internet, a modern version of the mail-order bride. Preying on such men, a trio of Russians plays a con game on the man, beginning with the fake website and culminating in the Brit stealing a large sum of money from the bank at which he tediously, joylessly works. The irony lies in the eventual, burgeoning romantic attachment that does actually form between the dupe and his alleged bride. What begins as a charade turns real: a slyly concocted love affair develops into a genuine meeting of hearts. Within this irony is a smaller one, involving the con game itself. The British bank worker is tricked into stealing the bank's money by the false threat of harm to his love interest by one of her accomplices in the grift. However, the accomplice is dangerously aggressive and he does, in fact, physically abuse the decoy bride. Consequently, the ambience or mood of the film is itself deceptive, as if we, in the audience, have been conned a little. What starts out as a quirky romantic comedy becomes more dark due to the physical aggression of the violent con man and the seriousness of the stakes for the Russian woman and the British banker. The woman is pregnant and the banker is on the lam, his future and that of his career looking bleak.

Con Game as Prelude to Love: Birthday Girl   75

Central to the unfolding of the legitimate romance is the way the dynamic of their relationship develops from surface facade to personal disclosure. The banker presents a curated version of himself online through the spurious website. After the bride arrives, the most revealing moments occur in their sensual coupling, but this is dominated by John's fetish involving bondage, another form of play-acting (since no one is actually hurt). So, Nadia plays along with John's sexual fantasy, all the while pretending not to speak English in order to make the con game more tractable. Nadia is also concealing the fact that she is pregnant, hardly a positive attribute in a prospective mate! Their life together therefore operates on the most superficial of levels. Rudimentary communication spiced up with intervals of sexual excitement.

But after the con game is revealed and John and Nadia are on their own, and on the run from the law, their time together expands their knowledge and appreciation of one another. As suggested, the searing criticism leveled at one another, almost perversely, advances their relationship by its candor, directness, and truthfulness. As in all healthy relationships, the criticism also furthers the self-awareness of each: John has to face that he loathes working at the boring bank job and that his expectations in regard to a foreign bride were, after all, unrealistic. For her part, Nadia/Sophia is forced to acknowledge that she was ruining people's lives with her perennial flimflam and that it involved her operating as a kind of call girl. In addition, working together to thwart Nadia's former colleagues and flee England strengthens their bond and estimation of one another's abilities. They become a team and this promotes the very romantic attachment that John had been looking for and Nadia deceptively insinuating.

Ingredient to the progress of their relationship are two cinematic devices: the symbolism of the binoculars and the trope of names or ignorance of them. The binoculars are placed in the story repeatedly to symbolize veridical perception. Looking at the other with the dual perspective of distance and intimacy enables John and Nadia to see "through" the veneers and charades that have characterized their daily knowledge of each other. When Nadia gives the binoculars to John at the airport as a parting gift, she is handing him her childhood talisman, replete with love and respect for her father, but also the lens through which she believes she sees the truth of things. When John subsequently views Nadia and her Russian comrades at the airport through the binoculars, he understands that she is now more a prisoner, subject to Alexei's volatile moods, than a willing accomplice. Without much thought or planning, he hurries after them, drawn by Nadia's compromised status within the gang.

The film also uses names, true and assumed, shared and withheld, as a trope for personal knowledge or its lack. Although John has always used his real name, he does not tell Nadia the name of his former girlfriend when with her in the woods. He has lied, however briefly, about her being dead and when questioned by Nadia, admits that he does not know why she ended their relationship. John's unwillingness to share the former girlfriend's name with

76   *Con Game as Prelude to Love:* Birthday Girl

Nadia aligns with his inability to explain his relationship with her. Withholding the girlfriend's name complements John's lack of insight: the unnamed is unknown. Nadia is not the Internet-ordered bride's real name, but she refuses to tell John her true name during their time in the forest. Only when at the airport, and an honest meeting of minds and hearts has been achieved, does she disclose that she is "Sophia." As it means "wisdom," the film is suggesting that she will share this most intimate truth with John when her wise judgment tells her it is appropriate. If John is willing to "trust and let go" of his former life to flee to Russia with her, Sophia wants to start afresh with the truth about who she is. As with the binoculars, her name was bestowed by her father.

Bibliography

Firestone, Shulamith (1989). "Love in a Sexist Society" (reprinted from *The Dialectic of Sex).* In *Eros, Agape, and Philia.* Ed. Alan Soble. New York: Paragon House, 29–39.
Lewis, C. S. (1960). *The Four Loves.* New York: Harcourt, Brace, Jovanovich.
Peck, M. Scott (1978). *The Road Less Traveled.* New York: Simon and Schuster.
Smoodin, Eric (1983). "The Image and the Voice in the Film with Spoken Narration." *Quarterly Review of Film Studies,* 8(4), 19–32.

Filmography

Butterworth, Jez (2001). *Birthday Girl.* U.S.
Dahl, John (1994). *The Last Seduction.* UK.
Kasdan, Lawrence (1981). *Body Heat.* U.S.

6 *The Game* of Brotherly Love

Love and Self-Knowledge

The Game (David Fincher, 1997) develops and reconfigures central themes that animate *Birthday Girl* (Jez Butterworth, 2001). The stories of both films are set in motion by love. In *Birthday Girl,* John Buckingham visits a website that purports to offer Russian brides to its clients. John is lonely and, despite the interest of a colleague at the bank where John works, sees no romantic possibilities in his daily life. In *The Game,* a very wealthy man, Nicholas Van Orton (Michael Douglas), is pushed into his topsy-turvy adventure by his brother's affection. Conrad (Sean Penn) thinks that for *his* birthday, Nick needs to be shaken out of a life devoted to amassing wealth. Where the quest for erotic love motivates John, Conrad's brotherly love is the impetus for the scheming that engulfs Nick's life. The upshot of both films is a gain in self-understanding by the protagonist. By the end of *Birthday Girl,* John realizes that he loathes the stultifying work at the bank in which he has been trapped as a result of habit and lethargy. Nick's wild ride on the "game" culminates with the awareness that his life is bereft of fulfilling personal relationships, so occupied with the business of money-making has he been.

The difference between John and Nick is that John's self-knowledge has been the fortuitous, unforeseen outcome of struggling through the con game played on him by the trio of Russian grifters. Looking for love in the wrong place turned out to open a window into self-awareness and, with it, the chance for real affection. For Nick, the gain in self-understanding is the whole point of Connie's con. He instigates the often-harrowing scenario for his brother in the hopes that by disrupting Nick's profit-oriented routines his brother will see the true paucity of his life. The two films also end in a similar fashion. Both men are about to embark on an amorous undertaking, "taking off" from an airport at that. Airplanes are transportation and both men, real and illusory marks of con games, have been transported into new and better lives. Juxtaposed, the films offer an inverted symmetry. John sought romance and found it, but gained self-awareness along the way. Connie aimed for Nick to become more self-reflective, and he did, but found a romantic interest along his way.

DOI: 10.4324/9781003364542-7

78 The Game *of Brotherly Love*

The timing is for Nick's birthday, but it is framed by familial death. His (and Connie's) mother has recently died and their father committed suicide at the same age that Nick has just turned, forty-eight. Along with home movies showing his father looking dapper at what appears to be a lavish birthday party, we are shown a flashback of a boyhood Nick viewing his father's descent from the top of a building. The home movie segments are interspersed during the first third of the film, suggesting that Nick is already taking stock, at least through memory-inventory, of his life and parentage. The game which Connie presents to his brother as his birthday gift is designed to create an existential crisis pertinent for someone poised between the demise of his mother and father, but frozen in a depersonalized world of high finance. And we watch Nick working: wheeling and dealing on the phone and in board rooms, listening to financial news, reading reports. Whether doing business with people or interacting with his brother and former spouse, Nick seems detached, unemotional, and somewhat arrogant. With the surprising embroilment of the game, a kind of pseudo-con, Connie also hopes to put a dent in his brother's chilling sense of superiority.

With the possible exceptions of his trusted head accountant, Sam Sutherland (Peter Donat), and supportive housekeeper, Ilsa (Carol Baker), Nick behaves in the high-handed manner that characterizes arrogant individuals. Arrogant individuals feel above other people. They have a dismissive attitude toward the opinion of others, while exalting their own views. For Valerie Tiberius and John Walker, people who are arrogant believe that they are better than most people because of their accomplishments or station (1998). The arrogant feel a sense of entitlement and corresponding disdain for others on the basis of their possession of "the excellences appropriate to human beings to an above-average degree. They take themselves to be more perfect instances of humanity" (1998: 380). As a paradigm of arrogance, the authors cite Mr. Darcy in Jane Austen's *Pride and Prejudice*. Darcy is contemptuous of the character and views of those around him because his wealth, education, and intelligence place him so high above them. Nick fits nicely into the portrait of the arrogant man sketched by Tiberius and Walker: Nick's sense of superiority is grounded in greater property or accomplishment rather than breeding or lineage. Darcy sees himself simply as "a better person according to general standards of what counts as a successful human specimen" (1998: 382). As with Darcy, Nick's grandiosity is based on his station, wealth, and the smarts he has used to attain them. Being worth hundreds of millions of dollars leads Nick to believe that he is "worth" more than those with whom he deals.

The inflation of self-worth that flows from some hierarchical advantage, however, is a mistaken inference; being smarter, wealthier, or of finer lineage does not make one superior to other people in a moral sense. In contrast, humble individuals have a realistic grasp of their strengths and weaknesses, abilities and limitations. Moreover, they appreciate that their achievement or position has depended on the help of others, natural endowment or simple

The Game *of Brotherly Love* 79

good fortune. Consequently, they realize that they cannot take all the credit for their advantages. Moved by a false sense of superiority, arrogance naturally translates into recognizable, high-handed treatment of other people. As Tiberius and Walker note, the arrogant person is disposed to the haughty treatment of others (1998). The deportment of arrogant individuals exhibits their condescending attitude and elevated self-regard. The arrogant person is convinced, as the authors remark about the lofty Secretary of State, Henry Kissinger, that other people should drop what they are doing so as to respond to his demands, that he should not be bothered with the needs of others and that his interests ought to be given the highest priority.

In his dealing with the venerable founder of the publishing company that bears his name, Anson Baer, Nick grows impatient at the older man's reluctance to see how seriously he has failed to meet his company's sales projections. Nick imperiously snaps at Baer for disagreeing with his stiff assessment of the publisher's business over the past year. Nick's behavior underscores how arrogant individuals are prone to lack compassion or understanding of others' circumstances or viewpoints as a result of their own bloated self-confidence and self-importance. Moreover, as with most arrogant people, Nick does not engage in self-reflection. So sure is he of the rightness of his opinions and judgment, Nick has little reason to question himself either in his particular decisions (as with investments such as Baer's publishing) or more sweepingly, about the course his life is taking. However, when Nick is finally humbled by the punishing hurly-burly of "the game," his demeanor changes, for the better. With his arrogance deflated, Nick learns to treat other people with proper regard and even manages to plead for help. His lowered self-esteem and loss of hauteur open Nick to the much-needed examination of the true quality of his life, especially in regard to his impoverished personal relationships.

The Game Is Afoot

Nick meets his brother, Conrad, at a restaurant and after exchanging some brusque words (including inquiry into Connie's drug-addled history), Connie presents his birthday gift. A card that signifies a paid "game" from Consumer Recreation Services (CRS) that will afford Nick "a profound life experience." Connie says that he participated in the game with astonishing results and Nick promises to call the organization although he "hates surprises." Connie responds, "I know." When Nick goes to the offices of CRS, he is informed that the game is tailored to each participant, "We provide what is lacking." Nick, of course, arrogantly pronounces his life is not lacking in anything. The game representative compares the game to an "experiential book of the month club." Nick is then subjected to a battery of physical and psychological tests and questions, whose length exasperates him. When Nick asks what the purpose of the game is, he is told that figuring out its purpose is, in fact, the goal.

80 The Game *of Brotherly Love*

The aura of the legendary quest sagas is thereby cast: the hero will come to some deep insight after successfully traversing the journey of his quest. Later, at his posh athletic club, Nick overhears members (who are nevertheless strangers to him) praising the CRS experience. They give no specifics, but when Nick asks one about it, he quotes scripture, "Once was blind, now I can see." We will later discover that these men are plants, whose conversation is meant to entice Nick into the game.

Nick is soon called and informed that he has been "rejected" by the purveyors of the game, a tactic clearly meant to pique his interest further. When he returns home that night to his mansion, he sees what appears to be a body, but is, in fact, a wooden dummy painted with a clown face. Upon pulling a red cloth out of its mouth, Nick finds a key attached (to be employed later, when the occasion warrants). A newsman on TV first speaks about Nick and then, improbably, addresses him. As a result of a miniature camera in the dummy's eye, images of Nick in his home appear on the television. Nick flies to an unidentified location where he proceeds to fire the head of the publishing company, Anson Baer, for failing to meet his projected profits. Although the man is the founder of the company which bears his name, Nick is remorseless in his derision and relentless in his decision. Nick's arrogance leaves him unwilling to find a compromise or avenue for the eminent, older man to maintain his position. However, Nick is unable to open his briefcase to present Baer with the severance package that Nick is insisting upon, and so the publisher is spared a few more days at his organization. Earlier, Nick's former wife had called to wish him a happy birthday and Nick was distant and sardonic, remarking that she almost did not call in time as the day of his birthday was winding down. It will later be clear that his ex-wife and brother are the most important people in his life and that he needs to reestablish a close connection with them both.

Once again, Nick waits for his brother in a restaurant, but Connie never shows up. Instead, as planned, a waitress bumps into him, making a mess of his expensive haberdashery. This enlarges upon the earlier scene of the pen from CRS leaking on Nick's shirt at the airport. He will get soiled, banged about, and totally disheveled as the film progresses, emblematizing the disruption of his neat, tidy life. The manager of the restaurant promptly fires the waitress and Nick follows her out of the restaurant when instead of a bill he receives a note saying, "Don't let her get away." At film's end, Nick heeds the warning again by pursuing Christine (Deborah Kara Unger) out of the ballroom where his birthday party is still in full swing. The attractive woman brushes Nick off as he tries to apologize for her job loss. The couple soon find a man collapsed in the evening street. The waitress and Nick wind up being ushered into the ambulance hurrying the injured man to the hospital, but when they arrive, there are no lights and the place seems deserted. Nick surmises, correctly and aloud, that this must be part of "the game." After escaping a stalled elevator, the pair find that they are in a CRS building. As they scramble, Nick

The Game *of Brotherly Love*   81

loses his (jammed) briefcase, signifying that he is, indeed, leaving his old life behind. Because it contained the severance package that Nick had summarily decreed to end Baer's career, it may also indicate the beginning of the eroding of Nick's arrogance as well.

Pursued by armed CRS security officers and an attack dog, Nick and Christine wind up on a fire escape whose ladder is inoperable. They jump into a dumpster where filled garbage bags break their fall. Along with not letting Christine (the waitress) go, this foreshadows another event at the end of the story: a similar, but longer, drop that Nick will make into a soft, bag-like platform at his game's finale. After the pair clean up in Nick's office, Nick puts Christine in a taxi where she confesses that she was paid to spill drinks on him. This disclosure about her involvement in the game's shenanigans is itself part of the scheme, making it seem as though she is an outsider hired to perform one act. When Nick shortly goes to an upscale hotel which he does not remember frequenting but for which he somehow has a room key, he discovers a fancy room that has been torn apart and upended. The disarray includes drugs and paraphernalia, and the room is strewn with incriminating photos of himself and someone who appears to be Christine. When Nick flushes the drugs, the toilet ominously overflows. Nick meets with his chief accountant and right-hand man, Sam, and publisher Baer at yet another hotel. Oddly enough, Baer is convivial and grateful to Nick for retiring him, however forcefully. Nick is taken aback by Baer's cheerfulness and we may later come to see the gain in Baer's apparent loss as symptomatic of what Nick himself might stand to gain should his own career go off the rails.

Nick returns to his darkened home, with psychedelic images splashed on the walls and music blaring. Conrad unexpectedly shows up and is distraught. He tells Nick that CRS will not stop hounding him even though he paid (for something more than simply Nick's turn of the game). In a frenzy, he claims that the company is unfairly coming after him. The pair drive away, but the car gets a flat tire and the brothers fumble about and argue about changing the tire. Connie accuses Nick of being withdrawn and of being in cahoots with CRS because of all the CRS keys he finds in Nick's glove compartment. After Conrad runs away, Nick gets in a taxi cab, but the driver does not take him where he asks to go. The driver soon leaps from the moving cab leaving Nick locked in. When it flies off the road into the river, Nick is trapped under water. Fortunately, he remembers a window crank in his pocket that he had stumbled upon earlier, thanks to the game, and is able to open the rear window and swim to safety.

Nick proceeds to the CRS headquarters accompanied by the police and finds it deserted; as in typical con stories, the trappings of the ruse have been dismantled. Of course, no record of the company renting the space exists and so it looks like a dead end. Nick returns home and asks his housekeeper, Ilsa, about his father. She says that no one worried about him and that Nick is not like him. Having gotten Christine's address from the cab company, Nick goes

82   The Game *of Brotherly Love*

to her house. While she is in her bedroom, Nick looks over the apartment, only to discover it is unlived in: empty pantries and refrigerator, fake books, nothing in drawers. Nick confronts her about the photos he found in the hotel room, but she deflects his questions and whispers that they are being watched. More CRS goons show up, peppering the house with gunfire, and the pair are on the run once again. After they get in a car, Christine tells Nick, "It's a con." Telling a mark that he is being conned is definitely unique to tales of grifting; however, if Nick is, in fact, being conned into *believing* that he is being duped, then the assertion that a con game is being run would still fall within the parameters of the genre. Only in this instance, belief in the con game itself is central to the duplicitous scheme.

Christine and Nick drive away, pursued by a CRS security van. Christine admits to being part of the game, but claims not to know anything else. She says that Connie was always in on it and conjectures that setting Nick up may have been the only way out of his predicament, whatever that entails. Christine suggests that the operatives at CRS have probably taken money from his accounts. Nick calls his Swiss bank and gives them his passcodes, which Christine appears to be memorizing. When Nick is dumbfounded by the news that his savings accounts have been cleaned out, Christine explains that all the tests he took at the CRS intake were used to obtain samples of his handwriting and to figure out the relevant passcodes for his finances. Nick calls his right-hand man, Sam Sutherland, and is informed that, on the contrary, his funds are intact. Before he can savor the relief, though, Christine accuses Sam of being in on the theft. Christine chides Nick, saying that it is only money, "Be glad that you're alive." Christine pops into a convenience store and announces that the snack and coffee are her treat since the store cut Nick's credit card in half, finalizing its invalidity. However, Christine has drugged Nick's coffee and he begins to pass out as Christine informs him, through a fog, that they have all the access codes and passwords they need (to rob him). Christine concludes, "It's done."

Rumpled and filthy, battered and disoriented, Nick regains consciousness in an arid, windswept foreign country that turns out to be Mexico. After a terse conversation at the American consulate, during which the official responds to Nick's fabricated yarn of being robbed with skeptical sarcasm, Nick heads home by bus and hitching rides. In a diner, he pitiably asks for a ride to San Francisco, offering $18.78, all he has left after selling his expensive watch (no doubt, at a steep discount!). The image of the bedraggled Nick, in a grimy white suit, pleading for a ride is that of the once disdainful multi-millionaire totally humbled. Having been shot at, apparently betrayed by his brother and top accountant, almost drowned, and now left filthy and destitute by the side of the road, Nick is simply hoping to get home and find some answers.

His newly-found humility is coupled with a renewed appreciation for his former spouse. When they meet at a restaurant at Nick's request, he asks to borrow her car and she agrees without hesitation. He tells her that he knows

The Game *of Brotherly Love*   83

why she left him and apologizes for "not being there" for her. Nick was not "there" for her, we assume, because he was constantly consumed by accumulating more wealth. He tells Elizabeth (Anna Katarina) that she is the only person he can really trust, and asks for her forgiveness. This earnest expression of dependence and remorse stands in sharp contrast to Nick's earlier supercilious tone on the phone when Elizabeth had called to wish him a happy birthday. Instead of brushing off her thoughtful remembrance as a mere formality, Nick is now sincerely demonstrating gratitude for her support and continued affection. Humble people are thankful and express their gratitude; whereas, arrogant individuals lack gratitude because they believe that they are entitled to the benefits conferred on them. Why be thankful to someone for bestowing on you what you deserve! While conversing with his former spouse in the restaurant, Nick recognizes on a mounted television screen the man who conducted his interview at CRS. The man is now hawking some product, performing as a commercial actor, not actually in the employ of the game company. Remembering the Chinese restaurant from which the interviewer had purchased the lunch he was eating during Nick's intake protocol, Nick is able to track down the actor, Lionel Fisher (James Rebhorn).[1]

Connie's Con Game Unveiled

With the help of a sham phone call to Lionel's wife, Nick confronts the actor at the zoo who is visiting it with his children. Brandishing a pistol, Nick forces Lionel to take him to the CRS headquarters in his car, saying that he is "Pulling the curtains back," to reveal the wizard behind the elaborate scheme that has ensnared Nick. They take an elevator to a floor that houses what appears to be a cafeteria arrayed with many of the characters who have peopled Nick's torturous adventure. Nick and Lionel soon spot Christine talking with one of her confederates at a table. Nick accosts her, pointing his gun, and she responds: "What are you doing here?" Nick says that he is "Back from the dead." Christine tells him that he is not going to shoot anyone, but another set of security guards soon appears. Once again, Nick and Christine are on the run, as the security cops open fire. The couple emerges on the building's roof. Christine demands of Nick, "What do you think you're doing?" Nick answers, "You tell me. Who's behind this?" Christine points out that the treatment Nick has received was not personal, "It could have been any asshole with a couple hundred million in the bank!" She appears to be perpetuating the notion that Nick is being conned out of his fortune.

Christine then pretends to be surprised at the particular gun Nick is wielding, saying that they searched his house and did not find it. On a walkie-talkie, she complains to someone of Nick's "real" gun, but then reverses herself and explains to Nick that the whole enterprise is fake, part of his CRS game. Nick screams at her, "Don't start with me now." Christine repeats that it is a game, mere "Bullshit," and explains that it involved "special effects, squibs

84   The Game *of Brotherly Love*

[simulating blood]." She tells Nick that they have been shot at with blanks and that when he went under water in the taxi, the cab driver was standing by to save him should he have been unable to free himself from the submerged vehicle. Christine cries, and informs Nick that the people on the other side of the door to the roof, trying to get past it, are waiting with champagne to celebrate his birthday. And this, ironically, is indeed the case!

But Nick refuses to accept this benign explanation and demands that Christine stop lying. He is still under the impression that Christine and CRS have emptied his foreign accounts of all his money. Christine yells at the people behind the door, who are using a blow torch to get it open, that they should stay back because Nick has a gun. In a white dinner jacket, Conrad comes through the door holding champagne, ahead of a throng of partygoers, but Nick impulsively shoots him before recognizing just who he is. Distraught and holding a flute of champagne, Lionel, the actor, says, "You shot him," and we think so too. He yells for someone to get an ambulance. Christine bends down and opens Conrad's bloody shirt; she looks at the blood on her hands as the actor proclaims, "He's dead." Nick cries and Lionel asks Christine, "How'd you let this get so out of hand?" Christine laments, "He wouldn't listen to me." Lionel then issues a pseudo-recrimination, saying, "You never, ever, let the mark take over," and proceeds to bemoan the inevitability of them all going to jail, for a long time.

Beside himself with grief for apparently killing his brother, Nick jumps off the roof, mirroring his father's demise. We are shown what appear to images in his mind as he falls: scenes from his childhood and father. When he does crash through a glass dome, he hits a big, thick bag, designed to break his fall. The event is a protracted version of his earlier, short jump from the side of a building onto bags of garbage in a dump. Several people brush the breakaway glass off Nick and lift him up. Conrad approaches his brother, wearing his squib-reddened dinner jacket and a smile. Nick is amazed and speechless. Conrad says, "Happy birthday Nickie." Conrad holds up a funny shirt on which is written: "I was drugged and left for dead in Mexico. All I got was this stupid shirt." Nick cries and they hug. Conrad quietly confides, "I had to do something, you were becoming such an asshole."

Conrad makes the celebration official, announcing, "Ladies and gentlemen, my brother Nicholas Van Orton." Applause breaks out from the large gathering; music, food, and drink ensue. Nick makes a point to sincerely thank a variety of people for coming to his party, thereby expressing a gratitude that had eluded him prior to playing the game. As indicated, arrogant individuals rarely feel grateful for benefits received or kindnesses shown; they are confident that such advantages are their due, since their superiority merits deference and commodity. But Nick has been humbled through the trials he has undergone playing the game, including erroneously believing that his immense fortune has been filched from him by the con seemingly played on him. Consequently, he is grateful for such gifts as his brother's love and

The Game *of Brotherly Love*   85

birthday present: both the game and now his extravagant party – mirroring the one with his father when he was a boy, shown in the home movie flashbacks. As his ex-wife prepares to leave, therefore, Nick graciously thanks her new husband for joining the celebration, and she kisses him goodbye, wishing him a happy birthday again. Nick promises to call her, "I really will." Affirming his intention to stay in touch clearly indicates that Nick is taking the impact of the game to heart, including Elizabeth's affectionate role in it, and that he intends to make a new start. He has learned to appreciate the people closest to him, both his former wife and brother.

Nick then rushes outside to catch Christine before she takes off in a taxi for the airport. Yet another allusion to a moment earlier in the story. Nick is heeding, once again, the note in the restaurant that urged him not to let Christine get away. He tells her that he wanted to say goodbye. Sitting in the cab, she confesses that her real name is Claire (not Christine). Nick suggests dinner when she returns from her latest gig in Australia, playing another role in some new charade. When Claire says that Nick does not know her, he asks her to tell him about herself. After giving a brief answer, Claire invites him to have coffee with her at the airport; although Nick looks away and smiles, we know that he is going to accompany the attractive gamester to the airport and pursue their renewed relationship.

Here, we have another echo of *Birthday Girl.* The relationship fabricated for the sake of the game that "Christine" had initiated as a fake waitress has been discarded, replaced by a reality that nevertheless discloses the potential for an honest connection with genuine affection. In a similar vein, the spurious Russian bride had been uncovered as a pregnant woman who, at the story's finale, holds out the possibility of realistic romance. The ostensible names, "Christine" and "Nadia," have given way to the women's true names, Claire and Sophia, suggesting that artifice has been replaced by reality. "Claire" indicates that Nick is finally seeing his life clearly, without the illusory status provided by wealth. And "Sophia" conveys that John has acquired some wisdom and that leaving England and his tired life in the bank for a new start with a real Russian bride, is a wise choice. However bogus, the travails that Nick and Claire have banged through as a team have deepened their feelings for one another, even as John Buckingham's and Sophia's very real struggles with Sophia's former cohorts amplified their mutual understanding and appreciation. Then, too, the airport. The couple in *Birthday Girl* are shown as beginning their new life together before embarking for a flight out of England and their con-gamed introduction. For Nick and Claire, the airport is indicated as the off-screen site of their reacquaintance and incipient relationship. In both cases, a con game, one genuine and one itself a sham, marks an entry into a new romantic liaison.

The similarity with *Birthday Girl* includes a gain in self-awareness as well. John comes to understand the emptiness of his life after he is virtually evicted from it, as he is pried out of his work, home, and country. He

86 The Game *of Brotherly Love*

faces the truth that kinky sexual fantasy had been a feeble attempt to fill the void of stultifying work and loneliness. John is unwittingly pushed out of his dead-end and deadening job into an uncharted but potentially joyous new life with Sophia. Even so is Nick shocked out of his all-consuming quest for money to realize the importance to him of his brother as well as his former spouse, including his deleterious role in the demise of their marriage. As with John, there is no guarantee that his burgeoning relationship with Claire will blossom, but playing the (ersatz con) game has opened him to that attractive possibility.

The ending breaks the standard con artist film mold in that Nick has not been fleeced, except for splitting the exorbitant bill for the whole affair with Conrad. It is also unique in having one of the characters (Claire aka "Christine") explicitly telling the mark, Nick, that what he is embroiled in is itself a "con." But the film and the con played on Nick do follow the familiar formula: excessive (albeit mock) danger and violence; a huge cast of characters playing a multitude of roles; elaborate sets (as in *The Sting*); riddles to be untied; and the spectre of financial devastation. In these respects, the film can plausibly be interpreted as a good-natured spoof of the standard con game story.

Along with Nick, we, in the audience, are fooled into thinking that a real con game is actually being stitched together. Because it is not, because what we see is a simulacrum of an embellished scam, we are being "conned" into thinking that a real grift has been sprung. In this way, the film can be seen as perpetrating a meta-con: conning the would-be dupe and viewers into believing that a con game is being played. Nevertheless, this con game has been arranged to add to Nick's life, not take away his wealth. And yet, in enriching his life it does take away something pertinent to his money: Nick's over-concern with his work and accumulation of fortune, which had been ironically "robbing" him of genuine happiness. This parallels our opening film, *Matchstick Men,* in that playing con games on people to steal their money had been at the root of Roy's neurotically-plagued, sterile life. The grift into which he is drawn by his partner was not intentionally designed to liberate him from his guilt-driven compulsions and teach him to truly care for and about another person; however, it does have these beneficial consequences. As with *Matchstick Men,* the con game that drives *The Game* evokes a gain in self-knowledge on the part of the dupe. Nick has realized a barrenness in his life, although not as stark as the void in Roy's. And, he is now valuing such relationships as those he has with his brother and former wife. Even as Roy has established a loving, domestic relationship with the lovely clerk from the grocery store, Nick is striking out on what he hopes will be a fulfilling, amorous relationship with Claire. The difference between the films is that Nick's self-awareness and change in life-course is the purpose of the con Connie has concocted. Roy's was simply a happy, unintended byproduct of the ruse perpetrated on him.

Note

1 Listings for the movie's cast refer to this character as "Jim Feingold;" however, in the film itself he is called "Lionel Fisher."

Bibliography

Tiberius, Valerie and John Walker (1998). "Arrogance." *American Philosophical Quarterly,* 35, 379–390.

Filmography

Butterworth, Jez (2002). *Birthday Girl.* U.S.
Fincher, David (1997). *The Game.* U.S.
Hill, George Roy (1973). *The Sting.* U.S.
Scott, Ridley (2003). *Matchstick Men.* U.S.

Index

Note: Page numbers followed by "n" denote endnotes.

Abagnale, Frank 3
anxiety, obsessive-compulsive 12–19, 31
Aristotle 24, 49–51
arrogance 24–25, 78–81
Austen, Jane: *Pride and Prejudice* 78

Bara, Theda 33
behaviors: obsessive-compulsive 12–19, 21, 31; violence (*see* violence)
Bennett, Joan 46n3
bewitching character-type 33–39
Birthday Girl (Butterworth) 4, 5, 19, 62–77, 85; con game 68–70; fresh turmoil 70–72; reacquaintance 70–72
Blood Simple (Coen Brothers) 46n8
Blue Angel (von Sternberg) 33
Blue Velvet (Lynch) 46n8
Body Heat (Kasdan) 3, 33–47, 58, 60, 61n2, 63; enriching bewitching character-type 33–39; identity theft and legal trickery 39–42; "Matty's" triumph 42–46
The Breakers 42, 44
Brookes, Ian 37, 54
brotherly love, *The Game* 77–87
Buckingham, John 5, 62, 77, 85
Butterworth, Jez 62; *Birthday Girl* 4, 5, 19, 62–77, 85

Cain, John M. 46n2
Catch Me If You Can (Spielberg) 3
Cavell, Stanley: *Pursuits of Happiness* 1
Chamberlain, Joshua 51
Chandler, Raymond 36
Chinatown (Huston) 46n8
compulsive gambling 26–28

con artist films 1; *Birthday Girl* 4, 5, 19, 62–76; *Body Heat* 3, 33–47; comeuppance and cure 10–20; features of 1; femme fatale 4, 6–8, 33–47, 52–54, 56–58, 60; *The Game* 77–87; genre (*see* genre); *House of Games* 5, 20n3, 21–31; *The Last Seduction* 49–61; *Matchstick Men* 8, 10–20; *see also* neo-noir film
confidence game 34, 58
con game 2, 6–8, 21; *Birthday Girl* 68–70; clever deception of 34; *The Game* 83–86; liberation through 9; as prelude to love 62–76; romantic love in (*see* romance); tutorials 10–12; and violence 4–5, 22, 30
Conrad, Mark 36
Consumer Recreation Services (CRS) 79–84
Cowie, Elizabeth 35

Damon, Matt 3
Dangerous Liaisons (Frears) 46n1
Dave 3; Reitman, Ivan 3
Day, Doris 38
deception 4–5, 11, 65, 67; authorities 74; clever of con game 34; discrepancy in currency 16; love and 7–9; schemes 14; self-deception 37; sexual 23; transactional 27
Derailed (Hafstrom) 5
Dial M for Murder (Hitchcock) 46n7
Dietrich, Marlene 33

90 *Index*

disorientation 36
Double Indemnity (Wilder) 33, 38, 46n2, 58, 60, 61n3
dupes 11, 82, 86; *Birthday Girl* 4, 5, 19, 62–76; *The Last Seduction* 28, 49–61; parallel 21–25

Elliot, George 20n5

family resemblance 35
fatalism 37, 38
female con artists 1, 9, 13, 17n1; *see also* con artist films
femme fatale 4, 6–8, 52–54, 56–58, 60; *Body Heat* 33–46; enriching bewitching character-type 33–39; identity theft and legal trickery 39–42; *The Last Seduction* 49–61; "Matty's" triumph 42–46; pivotal role of 35
film noir 4, 35–39, 45, 46n3, 58, 60; *see also* neo-noir film
Firestone, Shulamith 73
flimflam 4–10; *Birthday Girl* 63, 75; *Body Heat* 44, 46; education in arts of 26; element in 44; *House of Games* 22, 26, 31; illusion of violence 22; *The Last Seduction* 51, 53, 57, 60; vices necessary to 14; victims of 1; *see also* con artist films
formidable woman 35, 49–53
Frank, Nino 35
Frears, Stephen: *The Grifters* 11, 19, 20n3, 20n4; *Dangerous Liaisons* 46n1

Gaita, Raimond 14
The Game (Fincher) 77–87; Connie's con game unveiled 83–86; Consumer Recreation Services 79–84; love and self-knowledge 77–79
genre 1–3; pervasive themes 4–6; presentation structure 6; reconfiguration 8–9; structure of remarriage 1
Gettysburg (Maxwell) 51
Gilda (Vidor) 46n3
Godlovitch, Stanley 50
Gone Girl (Fincher) 20n4
Gray, Judd 46n2
The Grifters (Frears) 11, 19, 20n3, 20n4

Groundhog Day (Ramis) 13–14
gulls 2–6, 8–12, 14, 19, 22

Hammett, Dashiell 36
happiness 8, 10, 13, 63, 86
Harrington, Jean 9n1
Holt, Jason 36, 37
homoeroticism 56
House of Games (Mamet) 5, 20n3, 21–31, 46n4; briefcase discovering 28, 30; compulsive gambling 26–28; humiliation and humility 23; *Matchstick Men* and 21–25; moral standard 23–24; obsessive-compulsive behaviors 31; radical dependence 24; violence 22, 30
howdunit 1
humiliation and humility 23–24
humility: *The Game* 82; *House of Games* 23–25, 31, 31n2

identity theft, *Body Heat* 39–42
improvisation 28, 49–61
integrity, *Matchstick Men* 14–15
intellectual virtues 49–50

Kaplan, Ann 37
Kasdan, Lawrence 3, 58; *Body Heat* 3, 33–47, 58, 60, 61n2, 63
Kidman, Nicole 33
Kissinger, Henry 79

Ladies vs. Ricky Bahl (Sharma) 20n1
The Lady Eve (Sturges) 9n1
The Lady from Shanghai (Welles) 38, 46n3, 46n12–47n12
Lang, Fritz: *Scarlet Street* 46n3
larceny: Dave's lack of 3; women and 7
The Last Seduction (Dahl) 20n4, 35, 45, 63; Bridget's triumph 58–60; improvisation 28, 49–61; intra-marital theft 53–58
legal trickery, *Body Heat* 39–42
Lewis, C. S. 64
liberation, through victimization 6–7, 9
Lolita (Kubrick) 46n3
love: *Birthday Girl* 4, 5, 19, 62–76; con game as prelude to 62–76; and deception 7–9; looking for 62–65; and self-knowledge 77–79; *see also* romance
Luhr, William 37, 46n10

Index 91

MacMurray, Fred 39
The Maltese Falcon (Huston) 36
Mamet, David: *House of Games* 5, 20n3, 21–31
Margolin, Leslie: *Murderess!* 46n2
Matchstick Men (Scott) 8, 10–20, 27, 46n4, 86; con game tutorials 10–12; Frank's masterful con revealed 18–20; and *House of Games* 21–25; integrity 14–15; malaise of Roy's malevolence 12–15; obsessive-compulsive anxiety 12–19; story 15–18
McMurray, Fred 33
Memento (Nolan) 46n8
meta-con game 8; *see also* con game
Minghella, Anthony: *The Talented Mr. Ripley* 3
moral ambiguity 36, 43, 60
moral standard 23–24
Murderess! (Margolin) 46n2
Murder, My Sweet (Dmytryk) 36

neo-noir film 7, 8; *Body Heat* 3, 33–47; *House of Games* 5, 20n3, 21–31; *The Last Seduction* 20n4, 28, 35, 45, 49–61; *The Postman Always Rings Twice* 33, 46n2, 58, 60; *see also* con artist films; film noir
nihilism 36
Nine Queens (Bielinsky) 9n2, 20n1, 46n4
No Country for Old Men (Coen Brothers) 46n8

obsessive-compulsive behaviors 12–19, 21, 31
Out of the Past (Tourneur) 46n3, 47n12

phronesis 50, 51
Pippin, Robert 38, 39
Place, Janey 38
Porfirio, Robert 36
The Postman Always Rings Twice (Garnett) 33, 46n2, 58, 60
power: Cavell's incredible 1; improvisation 51; and intelligence 38, 39; legitimate 7; political 33; sensual 46n3; sexual 33, 49, 52
Pride and Prejudice (Austen) 78
Pursuits of Happiness (Cavell) 1

radical dependence 24
Reitman, Ivan 3; *Dave* 3
Reservoir Dogs (Tarantino) 46n8
revenge, and self-knowledge 21–31
Richardson, Carl 37
romance 4, 12; attachment 64, 74, 75; comedy 67, 74; denouement 7; illusion of 63; legitimate 75; love and deception 7–9; realistic 85; *see also* love

Scarlet Street (Lang) 46n3
seduction 35, 49
self-awareness 43, 73, 75, 77, 85, 86
self-deception 37
self-destructive habits 31n1
self-knowledge 5, 6, 77; love and 77–79; revenge and 21–31
serie noire 35
sexual intimacy 40
sexual satisfaction 39, 55
sham 8–9, 18, 26, 83, 85; linguistic ignorance 69; violence 11
A Simple Plan (Raimi) 46n8
Smoodin, Eric 62
Snow, Nancy 25
Snyder, Ruth 46n2
Spielberg, Steven 3; *Catch Me If You Can* 3
Stanwyck, Barbara 7, 33, 38
The Sting (Hill) 2–3, 20n4, 46n4–46n6
Sturges, Preston: *The Lady Eve* 9n1
Sunset Boulevard (Wilder) 46n11
surprise 2, 7–8, 10, 42, 44, 51, 63, 73, 79, 83

The Talented Mr. Ripley (Minghella) 3
Tasker, Yvonne 38–39, 54, 55
Taylor, Gabriele 14
Tiberius, Valerie 78
To Die For (Van Sant) 34
Tourneur, Jacques: *Out of the Past* 46n3, 47n12
"Trust and Letting Go" 66, 68, 73
Turner, Kathleen 34, 39
Turner, Lana 33

vices: glaring 15; of ruthlessness 52; virtues and 14
victimization, liberation through 6–7, 9
violence: and cheating 57; con game and 4–5, 22, 30; and grifting 11;

92 Index

House of Games 22, 30; illusion of 20n4, 22; sham 11
virtues 36, 55, 60; intellectual 49–50; and vices 14

Walker, John 78
Weil, Simone 23
Welles, Orson 46n3; *The Lady from Shanghai* 38, 46n3, 46n12–47n12

whodunit 1
Wilder, Billy: *Double Indemnity* 33, 38, 46n2, 58, 60, 61n3; *Sunset Boulevard* 46n11
Wittgenstein, Ludwig 46n9
women: *Birthday Girl* 4, 5, 19, 62–76; *Body Heat* 3, 33–47; and larceny 7; *The Last Seduction* 28, 49–61
Wonder Boys (Kloves) 31n1